Beautiful
THOUGHTS

Beautiful
THOUGHTS

By the Grace of God

MAAFA DALIT

For the rest, brethren, whatsoever things are true, whatsoever things are noble, whatsoever things are just, whatsoever things are pure, whatsoever things are amiable, whatsoever things are of good report; if there be any virtue and if any praise, think on these things. Philippians 4:8

Dedicated to my Saviour, The Lord Jesus Christ, Precious to Our Father, and to me. He is Love, Life, Light and Truth to my soul, The Answer to the prayers of my ancestors who prayed- "Lead me from darkness to light and from ignorance to truth."

Beautiful Thoughts

by Maafa Dalit
Copyright © by Mohan Mathews, pen name Maafa Dalit, 2010

ISBN: 978-0-9564732-1-9

Published by
Pilgrim Ministry
43 Wrenbury Avenue
Withington, Manchester,
M20 1DR, United Kingdom.
zionpilgrim@gmail.com
www.freewebs.com/maafadalit

This book can be ordered from the Publisher

Printed and bound in India by
Authentic Media, Secunderabad 500 055
E-mail: printing@ombooks.org

Contents

Preface

This book was originally meant as a collection of thoughts that would serve as a personal ready reckoner for my own Christian life. It is now being given as a token of my appreciation, first, to my dear son and my beloved wife, and thereafter to all my brothers and sisters in the Family of Adam. May we receive grace to live our life in such a way as to be found worshipping Our Loving Heavenly Father forever together in our heavenly home.

Thoughts are the stuff of life. God's thoughts of love and care to us are countless. The lines of the battle have been drawn as Satan is trying to drag the minds of men down to the pit. "An idle mind is the devil's workshop" is an ancient adage. In a world full of inventions of all kinds stemming from the mind, may all children learn that Justice and Compassion are the Crown of Education. God wants our minds. More than anything else God wants to have the control of our minds.

If God has our mind - He has our body,
If God has our mind - He has our emotions,
If God has our mind - He has our appetites,
If God has our mind - He has our time,
If God has our mind - He has our money . . . see the point?

The One Who Gets Our Mind-Gets It All!
All the rest are just the scraps. Our mind is the prize! Rabindranath Tagore rightly called God as the Ruler of the minds of all people. The battle is for our minds. Satan is seeking to steal the minds of God's children. Our heart and mind are the keys to knowing God. Only a mind stayed on the Lord can have perfect peace. A personal Sabbath rest is the road to God's perfect peace filling our minds! Sadly it seems that Satan has caught many believers off guard. While they carefully avoid many obvious dangers, perhaps the most powerful mind robber has been overlooked. Satan is neutralizing the power of a godly mind little by little every day through the onslaught of the media that overflows us like a raging flooded river every day.

Garbage in, Garbage out is a principle in computer science. The deceiver of the nations, the god of this world and the prince of the power of the air is constantly bombarding the minds of the people with his thoughts, through the media and the evil meditations of the unsanctified heart. The tide has to be quelled by the believer and the thoughts of God of life and peace are to be invited from the Word and Spirit of God to ensure that our minds are not conformed to the world. Christ of Calvary is grieved that He is not given the audience within the heart of the believer for which He died. If we would read our bibles with the devotion with which we partook of the Holy Communion, the grace of God would rule our hearts and grant a healing of the attitude, moving us to a higher altitude in our Christian life. The royal law of Christ is to seek the highest good of our neighbours and enemies-viz., their salvation and physical welfare.

May the 'dalits' of the world find increasing livelihood through more caring Christians. The poor do not only need books and beautiful thoughts. They need that empathic provision of livelihood that the West is still unable to appreciate. It is pointless to fill the world with books of Christian purpose when we do not understand the care for the downtrodden in our lifestyle.

On a planet of amazing plenty, absolute poverty is entirely man made. It is a sad fact that many good Christian books produced in the Western publishing houses are outside the reach of young minds of the poor nations, simply because they have been printed at high cost printing houses. I am indebted to the staff at OM

India for all their patience and assistance in getting this book printed at a low cost. When the rhetoric of Western churches is moved aside, we find a cathedral Christianity that is far removed from the down to earth reality of the Christian world in the global South.

Those who love truth will be satisfied with the abundance of truth and righteousness, says the God of Truth. He is the One who helped me to discover the painful truth of the abortion that I permitted, as well as the religious lies of Christmas, Easter etc.,

May the entire world come to know Him who is PURE LOVE. Love is indeed the greatest of all. Were it not for His Love, we could never approach His Glorious Throne of Holiness. I place this work of His grace at the nail-scarred feet of my beloved Saviour and Risen Lord Yeshua Ha Mashiach and simply say: I LOVE YOU, LORD!

Part One

The Christian Faith

The True God

Justice and judgement are the habitation of thy throne:
mercy and truth shall go before thy face.
Psalm 89:14

He has showed thee, O man, what is good;
and what doth the LORD require of thee,
but to do justly, and to love mercy,
and to walk humbly with thy God?
Micah 6:8

Learn to do well; seek judgement, relieve the oppressed,
judge the fatherless, plead for the widow.
Isaiah 1:17

The God of the Bible is the Invisible, Omnipotent, Omniscient and Omnipresent Creator God of Heaven and Earth. The Jews and Christians call God as Father. The Son of God appearing as Jesus Christ in the flesh, called God as My Father and Your Father, My God and your God. Jesus is Himself Lord and God.

Justice & Judgement

The God of the Bible is Triune and hence, Thrice Holy. He is gracious, merciful and full of compassion. He is the God of the poor, the orphan, the widow and the oppressed. To do justice and judgment is more acceptable to the Lord than sacrifice. He will not at all acquit the wicked and without (His) holiness, no man shall see God. A lot of people may not understand why God seems to be silent in the face of all the wrongs of this world today. Every mouth will be stopped and all flesh will be silent when God will finally arise from His holy habitation to judge and execute justice. Woe unto those who will fall into His Hands on that day! God is love. But when God swears, He swears by His Holiness- His Immutable Nature and for which the angels glorify God crying out that God is Holy, in the eternity of heaven.

Satan
Father of Pride, Murder & Lies

How can any being created by God really believe that he can defeat God. And yet he fools billions of people around the world into believing that neither he nor God exist. How foolish then, can man become, if he should ignore God who tells us in His Word- The Bible, not only about Himself, but also about Satan and Hell.

The world is entering more and more into the grip of Satan- the Prince of the Power of the Air, the father of pride, disobedience, murder and lies. As the Church, the Bride of Christ is perfected and removed from the world; Satan will give his power to the Antichrist and a world system using the commercial code 666.

The light of God has no beginning or end. But evil or darkness traces its origin to the point in eternity when Lucifer wanted to exalt himself above the Throne of God and gathered some of the angels of God in rebellion against Almighty God. Satan is neither omnipotent nor omnipresent. But he has hordes (millions) of demons constantly assailing the hearts and minds of Christians, as well as unbelievers.

Satan is known as the prince of the power of the air, god of this world and the prince of darkness. The angels of God fight with the demons to prevent them from harming people physically and spiritually. The mind is the battlefield where the Christian has to win the battle against Satan by the power of faith, the sword of the Spirit- the Word of God, and the might of the Holy Spirit.

Satan has convinced most of the world that there is no spirit realm, God or Satan. Considering the awesome testimony of visible creation to the power and wisdom of the Almighty God, Satan's blinding of the worldly wise, is the incredible deception that all of creation has come out of nothing. God is permitting everything including the operations of Satan, until such time as God has amply shown all creation the Source of Goodness and Truth. And who the Father of Lies is.

When Satan fell, he lost his innocence
but not his intelligence.
Trevor Knight

The devil is the most diligent of preachers.
Hugh Latimer

Satan knows the truths and eternal realities,
better than many Christians.
Maafa Dalit

Our arch enemy is going to be cast into hell
and it will take only one angel to bind him.
Lindsay Clegg

Man
A Tripartite Being

Man was created to be the dwelling place of God.
Maafa Dalit

As God is a Triune being, man created in His image is a tripartite being, consisting of body, soul and spirit. The world affirms the carnal senses and pretends as though men and women are nothing but bags of chemicals. The body through its five senses is world conscious and the Eye is the lamp of the body, 80% of the gate of knowledge. The tongue was created to praise God and the hands were meant to be lifted up to bless God.

The soul of man is located in the heart region and is the seat of the emotions, conscience, will, personality and is self-conscious. The soul seeks love and companionship from God and fellow men. Christ died just as much for all of humanity as for every individual soul, reconciling it to God, through His blood in the everlasting covenant.

The spirit of man is the innermost dimension, located around the stomach region, where God and demons can influence or control, to the blessing or detriment of the soul and body. Rivers of living water flow from this region of the Spirit baptised Christian. True worship is the spirit of man worshipping God, who is a Spirit, with the help of the Holy Spirit. The Father and the Son dwell in the Spirit baptised Christian, making his body and spirit, the temple of the Living God.

Bible
The Word of the Living God

TREASURE YOUR BIBLE

- *A manuscript should be dressed up like one's child.*
- *Should be guarded from all others like one's wife,*
- *Should be carefully treated like a wound on one's body*
- *Should be seen everyday like a good friend,*
- *Should be securely bound like a prisoner,*
- *Should be in constant remembrance like the name of God,*
- *Only then will the manuscript not perish.*
- *These are the wise words of the Teacher.[1]*

The Bible is believed by most Christians to be the inspired, infallible and inerrant Word of God that is directly revealed by God and able to illuminate the soul of man. It is Unique in its Unity it has 66 books, written by 38 men and 2 women, and covering a period of approximately 1600 years. It is Unique in its Content with an accurate history of mankind, prophecies about Future Events, miracles that reveal God. It is Unique in its Indestructibility having survived the efforts of many evil men and empires to stamp it out. The Bible is Unique in its superiority to other sacred Texts. Before the discovery of the Dead Sea Scrolls in 1947 the earliest Old Testament Manuscript was dated at 895 AD. But the Dead Sea Scrolls reveal that the 895 AD. manuscript was virtually perfect. This means that the scribes copied perfectly, year after year, the Old Testament Scriptures. After the Jews returned from Babylon, they formed communities of scribes to preserve and circulate the precious Scriptures.

These scribes, later called "Masoretes" were so careful that they wouldn't write a word or even a letter from memory. They would be seated in full Jewish dress after having washed their bodies, and if a king should come in and address him he was not to look up. After the scribe finished copying a particular book, he would then count all the words and letters it contained. Then he checked this number with the count for the manuscript he was copying. If they didn't match, the copy was immediately burned. In fact, the Masoretes destroyed all other manuscripts except their own and that is why we have so few Old Testament manuscripts.

The Bible is the most translated book found in its

entirety or in part in 2,355 of the approx. 6,500 languages that exist, available in whole or in part to some 98 percent of global population. The Bible is unquestionably the world's all-time best seller with an estimated 2 billion copies in print. The Bible was completed in its entirety nearly 2,000 years ago and stands today as the best-preserved literary work of all antiquity, with over 24,000 ancient New Testament manuscripts discovered so far (compare this with the second best-preserved literary work of all antiquity, Homer's Iliad, with only 643 preserved manuscripts discovered thus far).

The printing press wasn't invented until the 1450's, but we have handwritten copies of the Old Testament dating back to the 200's BC. Remarkably, these ancient manuscripts are nearly identical to the Bible we read today. As far as the New Testament, the Bodmer Papyrus II contains most of the Gospel of John and dates from around 150-200 AD. The Chester Beatty Papyri contains major portions of the New Testament and dates back to about 200 AD. The Codex Vaticanus, the oldest complete New Testament manuscript we've discovered so far, dates from 325-350 AD.

The apostle John, who lived with Jesus and learned from Jesus, penned five New Testament books and died in 100 AD. We have fragments of John's Gospel that date from 110-130 AD, within 30 years of his death. When compared to other ancient works such as Plato, Homer or Tacitus, that short time period between the original and the most recent copy is dramatic!

Of all the ancient writings, most scholars agree that the Old Testament of the Bible is the oldest of religious books. It was first written at 1000 BC through 500 BC and the words were given by God to its writers. In comparison, most others are relatively young.

- *Koran or al-Qur'an (holy book of Islam) written in 650 AD.*
- *Veda (sacred scriptures of Hinduism) written 500-1000 BC.*
- *Tao-te-ching (Taoism book of philosophy) was mainly written by Lao-Tse, who is believed by many to be the founder of Taoism.*
- *Baghavad Gita (Indian Epic poem) between 200 BC– 200AD.*

Over 300 prophecies were made 100s of years before Jesus, and all were fulfilled in Him. Precise, detailed prophecies such as; where He would be born (Micah 5:2), how He would be born, (Isaiah 7:14) how He would die (Psalm 34:20), etc. Sadhu Sundar Singh of India, a Sikh who burned the Bible, was visited by the Risen Lord Jesus the next day. People of many different cultures have seen the Risen Christ of the Bible.

*The only true reformation is that
which emanates from the Word of God.*
J.H. Merle d' Aubigne

*The Bible is a window in this prison world
through which we may look into eternity.*
Timothy Dwight

My conscience is captive to the Word of God.
Martin Luther

*Sin will keep you from this book, or
this book will keep you from sin.*
John Bunyan

---

1. K. V. Sarma, "Scribes in Indian Tradition," *Jagannath University, Jour. of Indology,* 5 (1992):88. Translation by David Nelson.

Christ in Vedic Scriptures

In the beginning, God allowed mankind to sacrifice animals, so as to make them understand that there is atonement for everyone's sins, as it is written in *"Thertiriya Aranyaka verse 3, Sarvapapa pariharo raktha prokshna mavasyam"* which means that the atonement is through shedding of blood only. Though the animal's blood is not a substitute, it was expected that man would repent and turn away from his sinful ways by seeing the animal, which is being sacrificed on his behalf. But mankind started practicing it just as a ritual, and thus came into condemnation.

If mankind were to be saved from this predicament, as *Thertiriya Aranyaka 3rd verse* says again, *"thad raktham Paramatmena punyadana baliyagam"* which means that-blood has to be through the sacrifice of God himself. The Purusha Sukta says, there is no other way other than the sacrifice of Purusha Prajapati. *Purushao vava yagna (Chandokya Upanishad 3.16.1)*, God, the Purusha is the sacrifice. In the Satpatha Brahmanam, we read, *"Prajapatir yagnah"* - "God Himself is the sacrifice."

In Tandya Maha Brahmanam of Sama Veda, we read, Sru: *"Prajapatir devebhyam atmanam yagnam krutva prayachhat"* – "God would offer Himself as a sacrifice and obtain atonement for sins". Satapadha Brahmanam says, *"Tasya prajapatir ardhamevamartyamasidardhamrutam"* – God became half mortal and half immortal". This means that He united in Himself the human and the divine.

The Sacrificial Purusha in the Vedas
The Rig Veda specifies certain requirements for the sacrificial Purusha.

1. Should Be Without A Blemish (Nishkalanga Purusha)

Kaatyaayana Srautasootram describes in chapter six, that the water and fire were to be used for the purification of the animals, since blameless (defect less) animals are not available in this world.

2. The Purusha Has To Be Separated From Others

While sacrificing the horse, the sacrificial horse is always separated from other horses. A bush of thorns is usually placed on the head of the horse of the horse to inform the people that this horse is separated for the sacrifice. Also the head of the horse is considered to represent the Purusha *(Sathapatha Brahmana 13th kanda, 6.22)*.

3. The Purusha Has To Be Rejected By His Own People

In *Itareya Brahmana* it is written that the sacrificial animal should be rejected by its father, mother, brother, sister and friends (2.16).

4. The Yagna Purusha Has To Suffer Silently

Rig Veda 5.46.1 says, "Like a horse I have yoked myself, well knowing to the pole. I seek neither release nor turning back."

5. The Purusha Has To Be Tied To A Post

In Satapata Brahmana it is written, never do they immolate an animal without tying it to a pole. *"Na varute yapaat pasum alabhate kadachana (III -7.3.1)."* It is important to tie the animal to a sacrificial pillar before it is sacrificed. This pillar is called "Yupastampa (sacrificial pillar)", which has now become a flag mast.

6. The Blood Of The Sacrificial Man Should Be Shed Bruhad Aranyaka Upanishad (3.9.28.2) says, *"Tvacha evasya rudhiram, prasyandi tvacha utpatah, Tasmaattadarunnaat praiti, raso vrukshadi vahataat,"* As the sap comes out of the cut tree, blood comes out of the Purusha who is cut.

7. The Sacrificed Animal's Bones Should Not Be Broken

In *Itareya Brahmana 2.6* it is stated that the sacrificer separates the twenty-six ribs of the animal without breaking them.

8.   The Sacrificed Purusha Should Return To Life

The Bruhad Aranyaka Upanishad says, *"Yad Vruksho vrukshano rohati, mulannavatharah punah, martyah svinmrutyuna vruknah, kasmaanmulaat prarohati, Retasa iti maavocata, jivatastat praja yate, dhanaruh a iva vai crau vruksho, anjasaa pretya sammbhavha,"* which means, if the tree is cut, it will grow again from its root. But after the man (martyah) was cut off by death, from which root does he come forth? This man (Purusha) comes alive, on his own.

Prophecy Fulfilled in Jesus

1.   Jesus Christ Was Without Any Blemish.

In the Old Testament Bible it is written, "Do not bring anything with a defect, because it will not be accepted on your behalf"(Levi.22:20). "Whether male or female, present before the Lord an animal without defect" (Levi.3:1). The New Testament says, "In Him (Jesus Christ) there was no sin"(1 John 3:5).

2.   Jesus Christ Was Separated From Others

The Bible says, "the soldiers platted a crown of thorns, and put it on his head, and they put on him a purple robe" John 19:2, thus separating Him from others.

3.   Jesus Christ Was Rejected By His Own People
The Prophet Isaiah wrote, "He (Jesus Christ) was despised and rejected and they shouted to crucify him". Jesus said on the cross, "Eloi Iama sabaktani", which means, "My God, My God, why have you forsaken me?" (Mathew 27:46).

4.   Jesus Christ Suffered Silently
"He was oppressed and afflicted, yet He did not open his mouth. He was led like a lamb to the slaughter and as a sheep before the Shearer's is silent" (Isaiah 56:7).

5.   Jesus Christ's Blood Was Shed
This was fulfilled in Jesus Christ when he was nailed to the cross. "He did not enter by means of the blood of goats and calves; but entered the most holy place once for all by His own blood, having obtained eternal redemption. Without shedding blood there is no redemption" (Heb 9:12,22).

6.   Jesus Christ's Bones Were Not Broken
In the Bible, Exodus 12:46 says that the bones of the animal should not be broken. Three hours after crucifixion, "when they (soldiers) came to Jesus, and saw that he was dead already, they brake not his legs"(John 19:33).

7.   Jesus Christ Rose Again From The Dead
"Him (Jesus Christ) God raised up the third day, and

showed him openly" (Acts 10:40). "But now is Christ risen from the dead, and become the first fruits of them that slept"(1Cor. 15:20).

Sweat, Thorns and Blood
The One True King

Sweat was a curse on man ever since Adam was put out of the Garden of Eden. Sweat was to be absorbed by the linen of the priests in the Old Testament. No sweat of human endeavour or righteousness is accorded any merit in heaven. Religion of any kind is essentially man sweating to please God. But the sweat that oozes out of the skin, stems from the sinful blood of fallen man. Hence, greater the independent effort of man, greater becomes the sin of man in the sight of God.

The average person has 2.6 million sweat glands in the skin. Humans have two types of sweat glands. One type is the eccrine, or sudoriferous, glands, which serve a cooling function. The sweat secretions which pass through the lumen of eccrine glands are never accompanied by cell secretions. The second type of sweat gland found in humans, called apocrine glands, are responsible for the production of body odour. The sweat produced in a single day on our feet can be enough to fill a cup! When nervous, anxious or afraid, there is an increase in sweat production on the palms and armpits. This is "cold" sweat.

Luke, the physician writes about the "great drops of blood" that fell from his brow to the ground. Cases have been reported of hematidrosis, a bloody sweat that emits from the forehead of a person under extreme emotional stress. When the tiny blood vessels of the forehead rupture from the stress, it combines with sweat and forms the bloody sweat.

The Only True King took my Curse upon His Crown

And being in an agony he prayed more earnestly: and his sweat was as it were great drops of blood falling down to the ground. (Luke 22:44)

The Greek word Luke used, that is translated "great drops," can also be translated clots. The stress Jesus experienced was so great, that his tiny blood vessels did not only rupture and form a bloody sweat, rather, blood clots fell from his brow on the ground. The stress was of facing death on the cross and taking on the sin of the world. The turning away of His Father's Face. The Roman Soldiers would thrust a crown of thorns upon His head, beat Him with a cat-of-nine-tails and thrust spikes through His hands and feet, and He would bleed again. But those wounds would be inflicted from without. At Gethsemane, His wounds came from within. The stress was so great, He bled "great drops of blood."

Blood is the fluid of life, health and growth-the average adult having five litres of blood coursing through the body. The life of the flesh is in the blood, says the Bible. Without shedding of blood there is no remission of sin. The blood of murder cries for revenge. The blood of Christ pleads forgiveness. The blood of Christ makes the eternal family of Jesus where all bend their knees to the Father in adoration of His Love that offered the Only Begotten, the eternally begotten Son of God.

The drops of blood at Gethsemane, became a fountain at Calvary, covering the entire globe, each and every sinful child of Adam. The bonds of this blood of Jesus are stronger than the relationships that are formed in the family of sinful birth in the bonds of sinful blood. The way to Heaven was opened by the broken heart of God and the gushing fountain of sinless blood of the Sinless Lamb of God atoning for all your sin and mine. It pleads forgiveness at the Most Holy Place in the Tabernacle pitched by God, in Heaven, and washes my uncleanness of mind, spirit and heart. God sees the blood of Jesus and imputes the righteousness of Christ to me. What an offer of love! The love of God is stronger than death.

Thorns were one of the curses invoked by God on creation because of the disobedience of man. The thorns on the crown of the Son of God stand for all my carnal, wandering, filthy and selfish thoughts. That the Infinite, Immortal God should love a sinful, mortal being like you and me to such an extent requires an eternity to appreciate.

God being utterly Holy cannot manifest His Love for sinful men without the equally extreme atonement for sin. Satan and his angels are not offered salvation and the angels of God wish to know more about this unique salvation and offer of grace that was obtained by the sinless flesh and blood of the Lamb of God, at such incalculable price. For Free! For me! The love of my father and mother pale into insignificance in the face of such love!

My sins hounded the Son of God to the dusty death of utter humiliation. In His death, I see a beauty that defies description and I am awestruck as I worship in tears and silence before the Majesty of God that became a worm for my sake. Generations have marvelled over this Divine Love portrayed on the Cross of Calvary. Little known and even less sung are the sufferings of the Saviour from the Whipping Post to the Cross where His form was marred beyond that of any man.

The Holy Ghost brought the Ultimate Sacrifice to the Father and the ugly form of the Sins of all mankind made even the God of Love to turn His Blessed Face away. Woe indeed unto those who will turn away from this Sacrifice that God brought to Himself. The heart of God has been eternally ripped open. Blessed are all who will believe my report. For they will see the Living God on the last day.

All the Way to Calvary, He saw you and me, my friend. The ransom of the Blood of the Creator is greater than the power of Creation. Apparently in utter defeat, the Lamb of God became the Lion of God to make a public spectacle of the powers of darkness in heavenly places. Every knee shall bow and every tongue confess that Yeshua is Lord and Emperor of Creation.

The Love of Calvary is the Song of Heaven.
Maafa Dalit

The Father of Love, gave the Son of Love through the Spirit of Love to bring many sons to glory.
Maafa Dalit

Who are the Christians?

*But I say unto you, Love your enemies, pray for them
which despitefully use you and persecute you.*
Matthew 5:44

I send you as lambs among wolves.
Luke 10:3
*Be ye not overcome of evil, but
overcome evil with good.*
Romans 12:21

*No comment could be more hurtful to the Christian
than the words, "But you are no different from
anybody else."*
-John Stott-

What the soul is in the body, the Christians are in the
world. As the soul is present in all the members of the
body, so Christians are present in all the cities of the world.

As the soul lives in the body, yet does not have its origin in the body, so the Christians live in the world yet are not of the world. Invisible, the soul is enclosed by the visible body: in the same way the Christians are known to be in the world, but their religion remains invisible.

Even though the flesh suffers no wrong from the soul, it hates the soul and fights against it because it is hindered by the soul from following its lusts; so too the world, though suffering no wrong from the Christians, hates them because they oppose its lusts. The soul loves the flesh, but the flesh hates the soul; as the soul loves the members of the body, so the Christians love those who hate them. The soul is enclosed in the body, yet it holds the body together; the Christians are kept prisoners in the world, as it were, yet they are the very ones who hold the world together.

Immortal, the soul lives in a mortal house; so too the Christians live in a corruptible existence as strangers and look forward to incorruptible life in heaven. When the body is poorly provided with food and drink, the soul gains strength. In the same way the number of Christians increases day by day when they are punished with death. Such is the important task God has entrusted to the Christians.[2]

If you were arrested for being a Christian,
would there be enough evidence to convict you.
David Otis Fuller

Church membership does not make a Christian,
any more than owning a piano makes one a musician.
Douglas Meador

Man must have God or an idol.
Martin Luther

---

2. *Letter to Diognetus (end of second century A.D.)*

Evolution
The Monstrous Lie

In the Image of God created He man.
Male and Female created He them.
The Holy Bible

"And in man is a three-pound brain which, as
far as we know, is the most complex and orderly
arrangement of matter in the universe." [3]

Evolution is not considered a theory any longer in the text books of life sciences. Even school children are terrorised to believe in the lie by teachers from their ivory towers. And to such an extent that Christians try to adapt the Bible to accommodate the lie of evolution. This blasphemous lie of wicked men runs the whole earth through TV and Internet leading many millions into eternal darkness. The lie of evolution, together with the worldwide march of consumerism and the respectability

45

of secular, atheist educational systems, is distracting the mind of man from the principal reason for his existence, viz., the search for, the acknowledgement and worship of, the Invisible, Almighty Creator God. God has no place in the world system of Satan that has derived tremendous mileage through the influence of Freud, Marx and Charles Darwin, all monkeying with the eternal truth that man is created in the Image of God. Random mutations cannot bring about the awesome order in nature. Information coding requires a Designer. Evolution is a gigantic lie.

---

3. *Isaac Asimov, Smithsonian Institute Journal: June 1970, p.10*

Truth, Power and Beauty

TRUTH
*Pilate told him, What is truth? And when he had said this,
he went out again unto the Jews, and told them, I
find in him no fault at all. John 18:38*

POWER
*Jesus told him,… Hereafter shall ye see the Son of man
sitting on the right hand of Power, and coming in the clouds
of heaven. Matt. 26:64*

BEAUTY
*….He has no form nor comeliness; and when we shall see
Him, there is no beauty that we should desire Him. Isa 53:2*

*He is the Lily of the Valley, The Bright and Morning Star
He is the Fairest of Ten thousand to my Soul.
-The Songwriter-*

The ancient Hindus knew that God is the personification
of Truth, Power and Beauty. The Spirit of the Lord one

day revealed to a child of God that all three are to be found in Jesus Christ, all three were fulfilled at the Crucifixion and Resurrection.

Pontius Pilate wanted Jesus to define Truth when Truth had taken the form of sinless blood and flesh to be crucified. Truth is not only an abstract noun, but it is a Verb and an eternal motor in the Person of Jesus. When the Almighty Son of God refused to use His power in yielding Himself to the power of darkness for our sake, it led to the Father swearing by Himself (because there is none greater): "Every knee shall bow and every tongue confess that Jesus is Lord." Every angel, man, woman, child and demon will bend their knees to this Name, in heaven or in hell. Crucified in weakness, He was raised in Power.

Jesus, the Fairest of All, made Himself of no reputation or physical beauty, yielding to an ugly death on the Cross, so that every soul that believes will see the price of true beauty, the beauty of matchless character- humility and holiness.

Peace, if possible, but Truth at any rate.
Martin Luther

The Eternal Reality of Jesus is that Truth is the Greatest Beauty.
Maafa Dalit

Better to embrace the Truth even if it kills, for the Love of God quickens the lover of Truth even from the dead.
Maafa Dalit

Death
The Last Enemy

Death is the surest thing in life to all men, yet no one prepares for it and lives as though it is something that can only come tomorrow or some distant future. Death came in the garden of Eden and was destroyed by the death in the body of the Son of God on the Cross of Calvary. The Bible says: "Prepare to meet thy God", to every one of its readers, every day.

Death of the body is not the end of the person, the soul continues in heaven or in Hades (place of darkness and torment for the unrighteous dead). On the day of resurrection, clothed with an everlasting body, every man and woman will either enjoy the sweet presence and light of God or be separated from Him in the lake of fire.

The best way to prepare for death is to know Him who destroyed Satan (author of death) through the death of His own body and live a life worthy of the mercies of God and everlasting life. Live each day, as though it were your last and clear your accounts with your Maker and fellow men every day.

Death is the gateway to heaven for the believer in Christ, every Christian can smile at death, knowing that Jesus will walk with him or her through the valley of the shadow of death. Angels carry the souls of the righteous dead to the gates of heaven.

Books in Heaven

And I saw the dead small and great, standing before the Throne, and books were opened. Also another book was opened which is the Book of Life. And the dead were judged by what was written in the books, by what they had done.
Revelation 20:12

The Holy Bible informs us that every thought, word and action of every human being who ever lived on the face of the earth is being recorded. The Lord Jesus Christ said that we would have to give account of every idle word that we speak! The perfect technology of Heaven will make a playback of all the registers and records when we shall stand before Jesus- Judge of the Universe. Those who sincerely fear God and seek His forgiveness will have the heavenly record of their sinful thoughts, words and deeds wiped clean by the Precious Blood of Jesus.

There is a record of the formation of the members of our whole being (spirit, soul and body) from the time we were fashioned by God in our mother's womb.

There is another book which contains the tears of saints (transcribed in some unknown language/form). The Book of Remembrance is one that records the conversations of those who feared God and reminded each other of the need to fear and worship God.

There is a book with the names of those who have received Jesus as Lord and Saviour called the Book of Life. There are books that record the secret works of people that will be made public on Judgment Day, when all these books will be opened, as also the Book of Life. All whose names are missing in the Book of Life will be cast into the Lake of Fire or Gehenna.

The only place outside heaven where you can be perfectly safe from all the dangers, all the perturbations of love is hell.
C.S. Lewis

The breath of the Lord kindles the infernal lake, and where shall we have engines or buckets to quench that fire.
Thomas Watson

Hell is yourself, and the only redemption is when you put yourself aside to feel deeply for another person.
Tennessee Williams

But I will forewarn you whom ye shall fear:
Fear him, which after he hath killed hath power to cast into hell; yea, I say unto you, Fear him.
Luke 12:5

Hell is truth seen too late.
H.G. Adams

Hell or Lake of Fire
Place of Eternal Flame, Torment and Pain

Having overcome death and hell, the Risen Lord Jesus has the keys of hell and death. The gates of hell will not prevail against the church. The first qualification of the citizen of Hell is that the name will be missing in the Book of Life. The wicked and all the nations that forget God will be turned into hell. Hell has endless capacity, like the eyes of man that are never satisfied or full.

Jesus said that those who say "You fool", will be in danger of hell fire and if the right eye, right hand or right foot offend us, it is better to get them spiritually made lifeless, than end up in hell with a whole body. Proud and boastful cities that do not obey the gospel of Jesus Christ, like Capernaum, though exalted to the skies, will be brought down to hell.

Religious hypocrites and their converts who have a poisonous inner life will not escape the damnation of hell. James the Just, said that the tongue sets on fire the course of nature and is set on fire of hell. The wealthy in this life who had no concern for the poor will burn forever in the flames of hell. The wisdom of God decrees that the feet of a whorish woman go down to death; her steps take hold on hell. Her house is the way to hell, going down to the chambers of death. Her guests are in the depths of hell. Satan, Lucifer and the anointed cherub together with hordes of evil demons will join the condemned souls of men when death and Hades are cast into the lake of fire. This is the everlasting Second Death, full of regret, fire, torment and pain.

The Golden City of Heaven

As you are reading this page, there is incessant worship going on in Heaven in the city New Jerusalem and Mount Zion with the sound of thunderous voices in beautiful harmony with the insuperable timbre of the music of saints and angels. The Love of Calvary is palpable as it streams with the light from the Great White Throne of the Father drenching every citizen of that great city where the Holy Ghost is King of Righteousness.

The Saviour Lord Jesus is King in Zion, where the once humiliated Lamb is crowned as the King of the Saints and Angels, in Unsurpassing and Breathtaking Beauty. The holy apostles and prophets who forsook their all and served Christ purely out of their undivided loved for Him are honoured by the Father. They serve those in lesser glories. As on earth, God is constantly drawing all of the celestial creation of saints and angels closer and closer to His Infinite Majesty; towards, and into His Wounded Heart of Love. Nothing in all the flaming worlds of God's creation can stand to compare with the ambience of love and holiness that fills Heaven. Hosts of angels suddenly descend from the City of God to merge with the worship by the saints in earthly realms.

O dear reader, may the King Invisible and Immortal-the Only Wise God, grant the mercy that we may prostrate before His Throne and enjoy Him who is Creator of Time, Space, Energy and indeed, the Fountain of all Goodness through the created dimension of timeless eternity.

See the bright morning
Dawning on the Other Shore
Where Jesus and the angels are awaiting
To lead us home
Beyond all tears and sorrow
To the bright endless morning
Maafa Dalit

And I saw the holy city, new Jerusalem,
coming down out of the heaven from God,
prepared as a bride adorned for her husband.
Revelation 21:2

It is not the place,
so much as the company,
that makes Heaven seem beautiful.
Heaven is the very Person of Jesus,
The Gaze of His Face.
-Maafa Dalit-

Part Two

Christian Values

Fear of the Lord
Pristine Treasure

At the end of the day, after all the church services are over and the Lord comes down with the sound of the trumpet, only those with the fear of the Lord or the Holiness of God can see Him. No church denomination, hero, or rule of life will help if we do not hoard this treasure that is greater than all the world's pearls, rubies, topaz, diamonds, dollars and euros. The fear of the Lord is a function of the very Spirit of the Lord that goes before God as 'Fire', devouring sin, and finally, all sinners. God is a God of Truth and without Iniquity. Just and Right is He.

No amount of culture, civilisation, education, qualification, noble birth or material wealth can buy this virtue. It is wholly and freely imparted through faith and grace to the child of God who takes time to wait daily at His feet, aware of Who the True Majesty Is.

The fear of the Lord is the beginning of wisdom, because there is no end to divine wisdom. We fear God because then we can be free from every other form of fear. A man who truly fears God is thereby one of the freest individuals on the planet. God dwells in the heart of the one who has a broken and contrite spirit who trembles at the word of the Lord. The fear of the Lord is a fountain of life to depart from the snares of death and the knowledge of the holy is understanding.

It is only the fear of God that can deliver us from
the fear of man.
John Witherspoon

Sincerity or Transparency

But let your communication be, Yea, yea; Nay, nay:
for whatsoever is more than these cometh of evil.
Matthew 5:37

Who did no sin, neither was guile found in his mouth:
1 Peter 2:22

Blessed are the pure in heart, for they shall see God.
Matthew 5:8

Crystal Clear In Speech And Life
Faking sincerity is a lot like boasting about humility!
To be sincere is to be real. To be genuine. To be honest.
And even...to be vulnerable. No easy task! Furthermore,
sincerity begins with something that cannot be faked --
honesty with yourself. A newspaper once printed a little
piece titled "Sincerity." It goes like this:

*"I wish I were **big** enough honestly to admit all my shortcomings;*
***brilliant** enough to accept praise without becoming arrogant;*
***tall** enough to tower above deceit;*
***strong** enough to welcome criticism;*
***compassionate** enough to understand human frailties;*
***wise** enough to recognize my mistakes;*
***humble** enough to appreciate greatness;*
***staunch** enough to stand by my friends;*
***human** enough to be thoughtful of my neighbour; and*
***righteous** enough to be devoted to the love of God."*

I may never be that strong, that compassionate, that wise or that loyal. But I can be genuine. The first condition to meet God, even before faith, is sincerity. Faith will never work without sincerity. A person who speaks something else than what he feels in his heart cannot be a trusted friend.

God and His Throne, the city of God, the gold and precious stones, that are made of eternal substance are all clear as glass that speaks for the transparent personality of the citizens of New Jerusalem.

Sincerity keeps the soul pure in the face of temptation.
Thomas Brooks

I know no religion, but sincerity.
Matthew Henry

There is no substitute for godly sincerity.
William Plumer

We are not saved by sincerity,
but we can be lost through insincerity.
Robert Black

Humility
The Divine Virtue

.....And being found in fashion as a man,
he humbled himself, and became obedient unto death,
even the death of the cross.
Philippians 2:6-8

A Prayer for Humility

O Jesus, meek and humble of heart, hear me.
Deliver me Jesus,
From the desire of being loved
From the desire of being extolled
From the desire of being honoured
From the desire of being praised
From the desire of being preferred to others
From the desire of being consulted
From the desire of being approved

From the fear of being humiliated
From the fear of being despised
From the fear of suffering
From the fear of being forgotten
From the fear of being ridiculed
From the fear of being wronged
From the fear of being suspected
And Jesus, grant me the grace to desire
That others, might be loved more than I
That others may be esteemed more than I
That in the opinion of the world
others may increase and I may decrease
That others may be chosen and I set aside
That others may be praised and I unnoticed
That others may be preferred to me in everything
That others may become holier than I,
provided that I become as holy as I should.
- St.Francis of Assisi

God thinks most of the man who thinks himself least.
John Blanchard

I saw seven steps to the throne of God,
each was marked Humility.
Pastor Paul, Founder of The Pentecostal Mission

God's choice acquaintances are humble men.
Robert Leighton

The humble heart is God's throne as to
His Gracious Presence and Heaven is
His Throne as to His Glorious Presence.
Thomas Watson

Temple of the Living God

A Murder called Abortion

In secret places, he murders the innocent.
The Holy Bible

God alone is the Author of life. God alone has the choice to terminate human life. That power is not vested in individuals or governments. The Son of God became a human being starting as a single cell- energizing the seed of the woman. There were 205,600 abortions in England and Wales in 2007. About 4,400 abortions were on under −16s. In a decade, the U.K. could overtake the U.S. as the termination capital of the world. In 2009, 189,100 abortions were done on women who had already had an abortion; more than 4000 women had had four or more abortions! Less than 1% of abortions were undertaken on grounds of risk to the pregnant woman's life or physical or mental health. 81% of abortions were done on single women.

Abortion is increasingly being used as contraception. For people of all ages and cultures, abortion is murder and self-restraint is the only contraceptive method approved by God. China has more than 13 million abortions each year as compared to 20 million births. Russia has had more terminations than births in some years. More than 35 million women are missing in the Indian population due to female foeticide or infanticide.

I am myself one who aborted our Down syndrome baby listening to the fatal advice of hospital authorities. The body of our baby was torn to pieces. After the murder, I was informed that there are women who would not mind adopting a Down Syndrome child!

God forgives those who genuinely repent for their sin. The world should not be rid of disabled children or adults as Nazis tried to in arrogant eugenics. Many who had out-of-body or near-death/after-death experiences and visited heaven tell us of an Infants' Paradise. Abortion is a crime worthy of eternal hell fire.

He that loves pleasure shall be a poor man. Alcohol-dependence and illicit sex have lead to the ongoing holocaust of innocent and unborn babies. In the world of high-tech medical science, the darkness is deeper than in the medieval age.

The Roman soldiers at the foot of the Cross were
gambling over the very clothes of the Son of God.
Jesus had to die to give us clothes that will never get
dirty or ever need changing in Heaven.
- Maafa Dalit-

Addiction: Gambling, Smoking …,
Problem gambling or ludomania is an urge to gamble despite harmful negative consequences or a desire to stop. Dr Jan Wise said that about 275,000 to 350,000 adults in the UK could be termed as gambling addicts. (www.bio-medicine.org 6/29/2006). In the US, state sponsored lotteries raked in 57.4 billion USD in 2006. Thirty percent of the profits from gambling machines come from problem gamblers (Wikipedia, 2009).

Many Governments themselves have taken on the role of being like drug dealers (CBSnews.com Oct. 31, 2007). Governments of this world are evil in generating revenues from sources of addiction such as tobacco, alcohol, gambling etc., God desires to make every human being his eternal dwelling place. Euphoric drugs, alcohol, smoking and pornography invite bondage, addiction, and demonic activity in the spirit and soul. Smoking is now well known to cause cancer, respiratory and coronary disease. More than 80% of the clients of tobacco transnationals are now in poor countries. Drugs destroy the soul and mind and the human being becomes a puppet for the evil adversary of God.

Alcohol- Demons in the Bottle

Whoredom, wine and new wine takes away the heart.
Hosea 4:11

The word "alcohol" almost certainly comes from the Arabic: al-ğawl, meaning "spirit" or "demon" and akin to liquors being called "spirits" in English. "Life water" is the name of several types of beverages, like Gaelic whisky, French eaux-de-vie and possibly vodka. The Scandinavian akvavit gets its name from the Latin phrase aqua vitae. Alcohol is the chief weapon of Satan to get demons into the city of your soul with the aim of breaking the family by possessing the tongue, destroying the brain and liver and to make you commit sexual immorality. Alcohol is one of the biggest traps that the Devil uses to drag humans to Hell. More men and women have drowned in alcohol than in the ocean. Teenage pregnancies can also be traced back to alcohol.

Production of alcoholic drinks is one of the rebellious activities of fallen man. In 2001, one person in 13 in

Britain was dependent on alcohol. Today, 23% of men and 15% of women are binge drinkers. Binge drinking women made up only 7% in 1998 and the rise is linked to greater financial security and the influence of advertising. The fruit juice of the grape that Jesus created from water, at the marriage at Cana, made them sober. The counsel of God to the wise is to avoid alcohol throughout our life. Jesus and His disciples will drink unfermented grape juice again on earth.

Ecology, Animal and Human Rights
The educated western and westernised world has set ecology, animal and human rights on the agenda in that order. Organic food is higher up on the agenda in Europe than paying a fair price to the producers of the coffee, cocoa, banana and other tropical products that are literally, shamelessly consumed for free. Custom barriers and other walls are put up by the European Union, Japan and US to keep out sugar, cotton and other products that are produced at much cheaper rates by the poor.

Human rights are addressed without any concern to the vast pockets of subhuman poverty and the rights of the poor. God says in His Word that He does not subvert the cause of the poor and afflicted. All iniquity will stop her mouth when God will show that He had sent rain, sunshine and sustained the vital force of life in such abundance, so that poverty is entirely manmade. The wastage of millions of tons of food on a daily basis in the wealthy countries is grinding the face of the poor in the dirt.

The pets of the wealthy are consuming more protein and calories than hundreds of millions of poor humans. Jesus was sounding the awesome judgement coming upon all coming generations of the pitiless and godless rich in the true story of Lazarus and the Rich Man (Dives). The walls built by the rich around themselves may well translate into an eternal gulf between the torments of the wicked in hell and the bliss of the righteous in heaven.

The man who lives only for himself runs a very small business.
Anon

Self is the chief end of every natural man.
Stephen Charnock

So subtle is self that scarcely anyone is aware of its presence.
A. W. Tozer

Shades of Corporate Selfishness

All from the loins of Adam
Created in the Image of God
We are all brothers and we are all sisters
One people made of one blood.
It does not matter with the shade of our skin
The tribe or nation we are living in.[4]

And having put on the new man,.....;
wherein there is not Greek and Jew,
circumcision and uncircumcision, barbarian,
Scythian, bondman, freeman;
but Christ is everything, and in all.
Colossians 3:10,11

Rabbi, When is it morning?
We are really not so different, are we? Old and young. Male
and female. Those of us from one nationality or another.
Those from one social class and those from another. Don't

we feel the same things? Desire the same things? And don't we laugh at the same things and have similar problems?

A wonderful story tells about an old rabbi who one day called his disciples and asked the question, "How do you know when the night is giving way and the morning is coming?"

One of the young disciples stood and said, "Teacher, isn't it when, through the dim light, you can see an animal and discern whether it is a sheep or a dog?"

The rabbi said, "No." Another raised his hand and said, "Rabbi, could it be that, when in the mist of the morning, you can finally look at a tree and know whether it is a fig tree or an olive tree?"

Again the rabbi said, "No." Then he elaborated:

"You'll know that the night has passed when you can look at any man and any woman and discern that you are looking at a brother or a sister. Because, until you can see with that clarity, the night will always be with us."

All men are born in sin into the family of (fallen) Adam
This family ceases at the grave.

Some children of Adam are born of the Spirit into the
Kingdom of God, into the Family of the Second Adam-Jesus.
This family lasts for ever.
Maafa Dalit

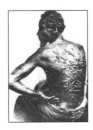

The human soul and spirit have the colour of the heart, not of the skin. The blackest deeds in human history have been perpetrated by a people who even unto this day call themselves "white"
-Maafa Dalit.

So God created man in His own image, in the image of God created He him; male and female created he them.
Genesis 1:27

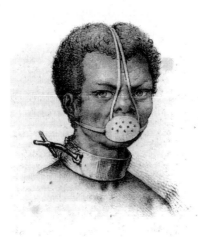

Tribalism, Nationalism, Racism…

Nationalism and religiosity have killed more people than this world knows of. In India, more than 250 million dalits (previously known as the untouchables) and over 70 million indigenous peoples are oppressed by a people who claim Aryan supremacy. Dharma Theertha wrote in his classic 'History of Hindu Imperialism,' *"No imperial power ever imposed on a weaker people a more ruthless and soul-destroying domination than the Brahmans did on the rest of their fellow citizens, and no race of superior men ever arrogated to themselves such haughty supremacy and false greatness as they have."*

Canada, Australia, Brazil, the USA and European Union are essentially countries with a murderously racist history whose hideous violence got them good portions of the earth's land and water. These resources are being maintained on racial bias while hundreds of millions are perishing due to lack of fertile land and economic opportunity. So-called Christians from Europe have even misused the Holy Bible to justify the Crusades, racism and slavery. The holocaust continues silently with the economic policies of global apartheid. In Uganda, Rwanda, Kampuchea, Balkans, ….ethnic conflict has led to genocide. Brother against Brother.

Non-Violent Resistance
Martin Luther King and Mahatma Gandhi learnt
from Christ the path of non-violence.
-Maafa Dalit.

For 30 years Rosa Parks bristled at the inequalities all around her. Her skin colour made everything difficult for her in the segregated South of the USA. On her way home from work in 1955, in Montgomery, Alabama she filled a vacant seat in the bus. A few Europeans boarded the bus and all but one found seats. The bus driver asked someone (meaning an African) to give up the seat. Rosa would not budge. Two police officers arrested her.

People gathered at Dexter Avenue Baptist Church to organise a bus boycott that made history and brought Martin Luther King Jr. to national attention. The 381-day bus boycott required patience and endurance as the organisers set up car pools to take workers who relied on the buses. The boycott succeeded and the Montgomery buses were desegregated in 1956. Rosa Parks and her bold defiance led to the civil rights movement of the 1950s and 1960s.

Martin Luther King Jr. paid with his life as price for his imitation of the non-violent methods of Mahatma Gandhi. Truth and Justice are as ancient as the hills said

Gandhi. Truth and Justice can never be destroyed in as much as God cannot cease to BE.

The Incredible Face of Oppression
As shown in the picture on the next page, African slaves were packed like sardine in murderous slave ships without passports and visas. The coffee, sugar, cotton and tobacco plants stolen from the tropics were cultivated with African sweat, blood and tears for the savages of Europe. Most of

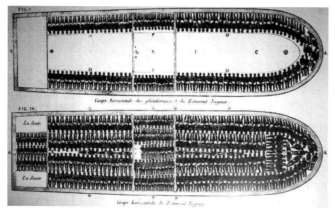

the slave trade was carried out after the Reformation. Every human child must be presented this heart-breaking story of the greatest holocaust in the history of Mankind as part of wholesome education. The anti-climax is the discovery that the loss of melanin, in so-called white people, is now believed to have been caused by a mutation in just one letter out of 3.1 billion letters of DNA!

Saddest Story in Man's History
The Industrial Revolution in Britain was fuelled by the wicked slave hunt in Africa and the tortuous journey across the Atlantic with the precious offspring of God. The Bible was misused to justify the slave trade using the Curse of Noah of his grandson Canaan, the son of Ham. This is the most ludicrous way to approach the Bible.

The toil of Africans in the Caribbean and the Americas created the wealth for almost 4 centuries for so-called Christian countries such as USA, Britain, Spain, Portugal, France, Holland, Belgium and Denmark. Now Africans fill churches in Europe as signs and wonders to prove that the God of the Bible is the God of Love. Africans have a legal claim over much of Western European soil and wealth, despite the European hijack of the United Nations. It is time for Europe to repent, make restitution and be reconciled to their African brothers and sisters.

Europa is the mythical fair daughter of the Phoenician king Agenor of Tyre whom Zeus king of the gods abducts on a white bull. Even today, the European Union (EU) is essentially an Apartheid Union that has created the Schengen Wall to keep out black Africans. This applies also for North America, Australia and New Zealand, as long as they continue to use "good white stock" and maintain racial bias in immigration.

Madison Grant of New York in The Passing of the Great Race wrote: "The cross between a white man and an Indian is an Indian; the cross between a white man and a Negro is a Negro; the cross between a white man and a Hindu is a Hindu; and the cross between any of the three European races (?) and a Jew is a Jew." The plain Alpha of the Gospel is that we are all the seed of Adam. Terms such as White Man, Yellow Peril, Black guard, Brown Coolie, etc., are all racist inventions.

---

4.   Songwriter at *www.onehumanrace.com*

Thoughts, Words, Deeds, Habits, Lifestyle!

You will keep him in perfect peace
whose mind is stayed on You.
Isaiah 26:3

I have been thinking recently about how important my thoughts are. I don't have to do wrong to get under blistering conviction and repent. I can lose the fellowship of God and sense of His presence and a sense of spirituality by just thinking wrong. God has been saying to me, "I dwell in your thoughts. Make your thoughts a sanctuary in which I can dwell. See to it." You can't do anything with your heart--that is too deep- but you can control your thoughts....

Your theology is your foundation. The superstructure is your spiritual experience built on that foundation. But the high bell towers where the carillons are- those are your thoughts. And if you keep those thoughts pure the chimes can be heard ringing out "Holy, Holy, Holy" on the morning air. Make your thoughts a sanctuary God can inhabit, and don't let any of the rest of your life dishonour God. See to it that not a foot of ground is unholy. See to it that every hour and every place is given over to God, and you will worship Him and He will accept it.[5]

"May my thoughts be a sanctuary this whole day, Father, where You can dwell comfortably. Amen."

Face Value, or Index of the Mind

Why art thou cast down, my soul?
and why art thou disquieted within me?
hope in God; for I shall yet praise him,
who is the health of my countenance, and my God.
Psalm 43:5

Ted Engstrom in HIGH PERFORMANCE (Here's Life Publishers, 1988) tells the story of a trusted advisor of President Abraham Lincoln who recommended a candidate for Lincoln's cabinet. Lincoln declined and when he was asked why, he said, "I don't like the man's face." "But the poor man is not responsible for his face," his advisor insisted. "Every man over forty is responsible for his face," Lincoln replied, and the prospect was considered no more.

Lincoln, of course, was referring to the man's expression and disposition rather than his features. A face conveys the thoughts and attitudes nurtured in a mind. We are responsible for how we will "face" each day.

One woman reported that she had just paid for some purchases when she heard the cashier say something. Not understanding, she asked her to repeat it. "I said have a happy day," the cashier snapped. "Are you deaf?" Earl Nightingale put it like this: "Our attitude is something we can control. We can establish our attitude each morning when we start our day. In fact, we do just that whether we realize it or not."

For the most part, you are already choosing your attitudes every day. Your ultimate happiness or misery depends as much on your disposition as on your circumstances. Face the day with hope and confidence, generosity and love, and you'll find yourself choosing to be happy. And you may be surprised at how much others like your face!

Rootage and Leafage

American President Woodrow Wilson once pointed out that "a man's rootage is more important than his leafage." What others see are the leaves, the outside. What they can't see are the roots, the values and principles that ground a person. Character is grown from a good system of roots.

One man of God says that the roots of a person are the thoughts, the leaves are the works. Paul discovered this and the mighty power of the Holy Spirit to cast down imaginations and high thoughts. He brought every thought to the obedience of Christ. People of character have both the strength and grace to give their best to the world.

To their enemy they will give forgiveness.
To an outsider, understanding.
To a friend, their heart.
To their child, a good example.
To their mate, faithfulness.
To their parent, respect.
To themselves, gentleness.
To all people, kindness.

Strong roots produce strong character. And a strong character is needed to give one's best to life. When the tree's roots are well-tended, the leaves will be full and healthy. A Christian is engrafted into the Vine that Jesus Christ is and his roots arise in the mind of Christ, while his words and deeds are the leaves of the tree.

Men best show their character in trifles,
when they are least on their guard.
Arthur Schopenhauer

The actions of men form an
infallible index of their character.
Geoffrey Wilson

What thou art in the sight of God,
that thou truly art.
Thomas Kempis

Verbiage and Literacy

As the face is the index of the mind,
so also words are the index of the heart.
Maafa Dalit

But let your communication be: Yea, yea, and nay, nay,
for whatsoever that is more than this cometh of evil.
Matthew 5:37

George Orwell pointed out 50 years ago, in his essay "Politics and the English Language", that slovenliness of language makes it easier to have foolish thoughts. We will be judged not only by our works, God will bring every idle word into judgement and our own mouths will judge us, our words will justify or condemn us. The bible says that the fool is full of words and that in a multitude of words there is no shortage of evil.

Jesus said that the words that come out of a man cause spiritual defilement of the heart, conscience, spirit and flesh, a defilement that matters more than physical uncleanness or pharisaic kitchen hygiene. Spirits of profanity fill the world as the ungodly generation curse God and godliness.

Among the many books being recorded in heaven, there is a book of the words we have ever spoken. It is good to repent for all our hasty and excess speech of the past and seek to minister grace to the hearers through our words. God advises us through Isaiah that we let Him wake us up early and give us words of comfort to speak to him that is weary. Peter, the apostle who once cursed and swore, on being confirmed later, urges us to speak as the oracles of God.

"The greatest miracle of our generation is literacy," says missionary Milton Martin. "Over 3 million new people learn to read every 7 days. They will read something - anything! They will be reached, and it is simply a question of who will reach them first." On the other hand, about 20 million words are being published every day in science and technology. India is the home of the largest number of the world's illiterate and most of them are women.

---

5. *Tozer on Worship & Entertainment, 10-11.*

Love or Lust

"*I could not distinguish between the clear shining of affection and the darkness of lust,*" Augustine later recalled. "*I could not keep within the kingdom of light, where friendship binds soul to soul... And so I polluted the brook of friendship with the sewage of lust.*" [6]

Life or Corruption

One symptom of the fact that the individual has lost the power to resist is shown by the sexual need of our time. This need reveals the complete uncertainty of men and women in facing the demands of his organic nature. The cause of the trouble is not the strength of the natural impulses, but the fact that modern man does not know any reason why he or she should resist them at all. His destructive doubt in the rightness of the demands of the Spirit enervates or weakens the will, and once this happens, the way is easily cleared for sexual impulses.

While a sinful man may use his mind for lustful imaginations, a vain woman may be inclined to romantic wanderings. Men, women, and even children are influenced by the power of demons that influence their bodily functions. While the motherly instinct comes naturally to most women, many men are inclined to believe that their urge and fantasies are just natural impulses of their sexuality. Demons induce and influence sensual lusting through their powers of darkness in the mind, as much as in the flesh. Even the medical professional ought to know that lustful thoughts fuel testosterone dynamics. To make things so much more complicated, in an age where television and internet content are charged with pornography, even so-called Christian women are foolish, or even wicked, to think that it is perfectly normal to beautify the exterior and make themselves sensually attractive with make up and ornaments.

Empathy-The Love of Calvary

"The Little Boy and the Old Man."
Said the little boy, "Sometimes I drop my spoon."
Said the little old man, "I do that too."
The little boy whispered, "I wet my pants."
"I do that too," laughed the little old man.
Said the little boy, "I often cry."

The old man nodded, "So do I."
"But worst of all," said the boy, "it seems
Grown-ups don't pay attention to me."
And he felt the warmth of a wrinkled old hand.
"I know what you mean," said the little old man.

The atonement mediated by Christ at Gethsemane and the Cross of Calvary was one of greatest empathy. He made our sin and sickness to come upon His body and freely granted us His own character of perfect righteousness before God. The commandment of Christ to love our neighbour was to love to the extent we love ourselves. Again, one of empathy.

Eduardo Galeano says: "I don't believe in charity. I believe in solidarity. Charity is so vertical. It goes from the top to the bottom. Solidarity is horizontal. It respects the other person and learns from the other. I have a lot to learn from other people." Jesus showed solidarity with the poor in condescending to the lowest rung of poverty, of being an outcaste and laid as a baby in a manger. Joseph of Arimathea understood true riches when he gave his own grave for Jesus to be buried in.

The ability to identify with others is a trait which, with practice, can be learned. Employers and employees are valued more highly when they posses it. Family and friends create more intimate relationships when those bonds are built around an ability to truly identify with one another. Chesterfield said, "You must look into people, as well as at them." It is a rare friend who has cultivated the ability to clearly see inside others and thereby identify with them. But it is a necessary part of an effective life.

Friendship is Everything

> *Greater love has no man than that*
> *a man lay down his life for his friends.*
> *John 15:13*

One day, when I was a freshman in high school, I saw a kid from my class walking home from school. His name was Kyle. It looked like he was carrying all of his books. I thought to myself, "Why would anyone bring home all his books on a Friday? He must really be a nerd." I saw a bunch of kids running toward him. They ran at him, knocking all his books out of his arms and tripping him so he landed in the dirt. His glasses went flying. My heart went out to him. So, I jogged over to Kyle and as he crawled around looking for his glasses, I saw a tear in his eye. As I handed him his glasses, he looked at me and said, "Hey thanks!" There was a big grateful smile on his face. I helped him pick up his books. I found out that we where neighbours. Over the next four years we became best friends.

Come graduation day, Kyle revealed a closely kept secret. "Graduation is a time to thank those who helped you make it through those tough years. Your parents, teachers …but mostly your friends." I looked on in disbelief as he told the story of the time we first met. He had planned to kill himself over the weekend. He was carrying his books home so that his Mum would not have to do it. "My friend saved me from doing the unspeakable." I heard the gasp go through the crowd. Kyle's Dad and Mom looked at me. Their tearful smile spoke volumes. Silently.

What would you Die for?

Do you know what you would die for? An ancient story tells of two great warriors, Cyrus and Cagular. Cyrus was the emperor of Persia and Cagular was a little-known chieftain who consistently repelled Cyrus' attacks. Cagular's troops tore the Persian army apart time and time again as they resisted Cyrus' attempts to expand his southern border. Finally, Cyrus amassed his whole army, surrounded Cagular, captured him, and brought him to the capital for trial and execution. On the day of the trial, Cagular and his family were brought to the judgment chamber. The six feet tall Cagular boldly faced the throne and impressed Cyrus.

"What would you do should I spare your life?" the emperor asked. "Your majesty, If you spared my life, I would return home and remain your obedient servant as long as I live." "What would you do if I spared the life of your wife?" Cyrus questioned. "Your majesty, if you spared the life of my wife, I would die for you." So moved was Cyrus by his answer that he freed Cagular and his wife.

On the trip home, Cagular enthused to his wife, "Did you notice the marble entrance to the palace? Did you see the corridor to the throne room? Did you see the throne. It was made of one lump of solid gold!" His wife appreciated her husband's excitement, but admitted, "I really didn't notice any of that." "Well," Cagular asked, "What did you see?" She looked seriously into his eyes. "I beheld only the face of the man who said he would die for me."

God is Love.
He who dwells in Love, dwells in God
and God dwells in him.

Meditation:
Do you know what you would die for? Loved ones? Home? Country? Faith? Liberty? Love? Determine what you will die for, and you will have identified what you should live for. Live for the few things you'd die for and you will be fully alive! Live for the One who Died for you.

Died He for me who caused His Pain
For me, who Him to Death pursued
Amazing Love, How can it be
That thou my God should die for me!
-Hymnwriter-

We must not think that our love has to be extraordinary. But we do need to love without getting tired. How does a lamp burn? Through the continuous input of small drops of oil. These drops are the small things of daily life: faithfulness, small words of kindness, a thought for others, our way of being quiet, of looking, of speaking, and of acting. They are the true drops of love that keep our lives and relationships burning like a lively flame. -Mother Teresa.

The Driving Factor

If you don't know where you are going, you might wind up someplace else." There is something to be said for knowing where you're going. But even if you know where you want to end up, do you REALLY WANT to go there? Is the dream you are following IMPORTANT to you? Motivator Tony Robbins says, "People are not lazy. They simply have impotent goals -- that is, goals that do not inspire them." They don't accomplish what they set out to do because they lose interest. Their dream, their goal, is really not that important to them.

A Christian went to Abbot Goeschel and asked, "Please, tell me how I can protect my soul from the snares of the devil." Goeschel lit a candle and told him, "Put your hand over the flame." "Oh, no," said the man. "The flame is so hot that it would burn my fingers." Goeschel said: Anyone who wishes to be unconquered by evil must first enkindle the flame of love in one's heart. The devil cannot touch a soul afire with love.

Think of Dennis Oehler. He ran the 100-meter dash in 11.73 seconds. Record-holder Carl Lewis ran it in 9.92 seconds, a full 1.8 seconds faster. So what's the big deal? Carl Lewis has two legs. Dennis Oehler has one. One leg... and a huge dream. Writer Tim Redmond says this about following worthwhile goals: "There are many things that will catch my eye, but there are only a few that catch my heart...it is those I consider to pursue."

If you work at love, you will find love at work.
Peter Jackson

Even the heart of God thirsts after love.
Abraham Kuyper

We are shaped and fashioned by what we love.
Johann von Goethe

The proof of love is its capacity to suffer
for its object of affection.
Anon

---

6. *Augustine of Hippo, Saint (354-430) bishop of Hippo (in Algeria, 396-430) noted for his writings as the autobiographical Confessions and the City of God.*

Forgiveness

*For if you forgive men their trespasses,
your heavenly Father will also forgive you:
But if you forgive not men their trespasses,
neither will your Father forgive your trespasses.
Matthew 6:14*

A beautiful legend tells of an African tribe that ritualises forgiveness. When a tribe member acts irresponsibly or unjustly, he/she is taken to the centre of the village. All work ceases and every man, woman and child in the village gathers in a large circle around the accused. Then the tribe bombards the rejected person with affirmations! One at a time, friends and family enumerate all the good the individual has done.

Every incident, every experience that can be recalled with some detail and accuracy is recounted. All their positive attributes, strengths and kindnesses are recited carefully and at length. Finally, the tribal circle is broken, a joyous celebration takes place, and the outcast is welcomed back into the tribe.

What a beautiful ritual of restoration! They replace hurt with happiness; pain with peace. Once again they are family. The rejected one is restored and the village is made whole. Paul Boese has said, "Forgiveness does not change the past, but it does enlarge the future."

"Forgiveness is the key that unlocks the door of resentment and the handcuffs of hate. It is a power that breaks the chains of bitterness and the shackles of selfishness." These were the words of Corrie Ten Boom, who as a young woman was imprisoned in a Nazi Concentration Camp during II World War. The weak can never forgive. Forgiveness is the attribute of the strong. I can forgive but I can't forget" is only another way of saying "I cannot forgive."

"One of the things, I've learned as a psychotherapist
is that Forgiveness: the need to forgive others
and the need to be forgiven,
has incredible healing effects."
Sister Bernadette Heslin

God never forgives sin, without changing the
nature of the sinner.
Iain H. Murray

What man uncovers, God will cover,
What man covers, God will uncover.
Anon

Those who say they will forgive, but cannot forget,
simply bury the hatchet, but leave the handle out
for immediate use.
D.L. Moody

You never so touch the ocean of God's love as when
you forgive and love your enemies.
Corrie Ten Boom

Peace or Pieces

Great peace have they which love thy law:
and nothing shall offend them.
Psalm 119:165

There is no peace, says the LORD, unto the wicked.
Isaiah 48:22

Blessed are the peacemakers,
for they shall be called the children of God.
Matthew 5:9

Like Adam after the Fall, every person without a living relationship restored by Jesus Christ with the Living God does not have peace or a clean conscience. Where there was perfect peace and harmony in the Garden of Eden, everything went to pieces and disharmony. Faith in the atonement of Jesus Christ, Son of God at the Cross of Calvary has brought peace to untold millions. Even wild animals can sense the peace of Jesus in the heart of a sanctified child of God.

Experiencing the forgiveness of God imparts peace to the troubled soul. When we forgive those who hurt us, we find the key to our own personal peace. God keeps them in perfect peace whose minds are stayed on Him. Great peace have they who love the law of God and nothing shall offend them. We are urged by the Psalmist to seek peace and pursue it.

The Lord Jesus has made peace for us through His atoning blood and His death on the Cross, destroying him that had the power of death. Jesus has left His Peace with us. So He asked us not to let our heart be troubled, nor be afraid. Before His death, Jesus told the disciples: My peace I give to you, not as the world gives. After His resurrection, when the Prince of Peace appeared to His disciples, He said: Peace be unto you.

Peace flows from purity.
Thomas Watson

Stayed upon Jehovah, Hearts are fully blest
Finding as He promised Perfect peace and rest.
Frances Ridley Havergal

Peace is such a precious jewel that I would
give anything for it but truth.
Matthew Henry

Peace is the Smile of God reflected in the soul of the believer.
William Hendriksen

Job's Virtue
Sterling Faithfulness

Well done, thou good and faithful servant,
Enter thou into the joy of thy Lord.
Matthew 25:23

And righteousness shall be the girdle of his loins,
and faithfulness the girdle of his reins.
Isaiah 11:5

Loss of all his property, his children and his health was the price of Job's faithfulness in prosperity. But abiding faithful, he saw a greater end after the trial of faith. Imprisonment was the reward for the purity and faithfulness of Joseph. Good men are few, faithful men are fewer and holy men of God are rare. Paul says that God considered him faithful and put him in the ministry and that he received mercy to be faithful. Joseph and Daniel were faithful in foreign lands and despite the peer pressure that they underwent.

The faithful can finish their race and hear the words of Jesus: Well done, thou Good and faithful servant. He that is faithful in the least is also faithful in much and he that is faithful in God-given resources will be given a reward that will be several times greater in magnitude. King Solomon said: Every man will boast of his own goodness, but a faithful man who can find. Faithfulness touches the heart of God for all of His creation, despite the Fall of man, reflect the faithfulness of God. Loyalty to God may require a man to stand alone in a crowd, in a whole country or the whole world.

Time is Running Out

One morning in 1888, Alfred Nobel, inventor of dynamite, the man who had spent his life amassing a fortune from the manufacture and sale of weapons of destruction, awoke to read his own obituary. Alfred's brother had died, and the reporter inadvertently wrote Alfred's obituary. Alfred read the obituary with horror.

For the first time, Alfred Nobel saw himself as the world saw himsimply a merchant of death. He felt that the world must know the true meaning and purpose of his life! He resolved to do this through his last will and testament. The final disposition of his fortune would show the world his life's ideals. And at that time came into being yearly prizes for chemistry, physics, medicine, literature- and the famous Nobel Peace Prize. If you were to read your own obituary today, what would it say? Few of us want fame, most of us do not expect to make a worldwide impact. But do others know what you stand for, what you believe in, and what truly matters to you?

"What remarkable, extraordinary and amazing things will you do with this wonderful miracle, your one and only life?" The question should perhaps also be asked this way: "What will you do with this wonderful miracle, your one and only DAY?" How we spend our days will decide how we spend our lives. But you have already begun to write it -- day by day, moment by moment. Live your todays as if they truly matter, and tomorrow you will look back on a life that counted.

Patience forms Character

Suffering in the will of God through Time = Patience of the saints. Like a pearl or diamond, this virtue is formed through time. When the character of Jesus is formed in a Christian, the glory in heaven will reflect the process through which the character was formed. The gates of New Jerusalem are 'pearls' showing how the entrance to eternal life is obtained through many trials and tribulations. —Maafa Dalit

Impatience is the mark of the sinner- both in feet that hasten to sin and a fool that is full of words. But if we hope for that we see not, then do we with patience wait for it. The patience of the saints of God is the endurance that enables them to receive the end of their faith, even the salvation of our souls. Tribulation works patience, experience and hope. The virtue of patience becomes stronger through time, testing and waiting on God. The end of the trial will always reveal that the Lord is pitiful and full of tender mercy as the patience of Job. Faithful Abraham was blessed in being patient in the promise that God had given him through twenty five years. Patience is not passive, but the active abiding in faith, while giving glory to God. Patience is waiting on God daily through a whole lifetime. It is good for a man that he should both hope and quietly wait for His God. The patience of the saints is associated with the mark (nature) of the beast 666 (covetousness) that the saints refuse to accept on their forehead (minds) or right hands (deeds). Patience of the saints is the very faith of Jesus, that can require martyrdom in consummation.

Courtesy

A wonderful story comes from 19th Century England. According to the account, Queen Victoria was once at a diplomatic reception in London. The guest of honour was an African chieftain. All went well during the meal until, at the end, finger bowls were served. The guest of honour had never seen a British finger bowl, and no one had thought to brief him beforehand about its purpose. So he took the bowl in his two hands, lifted it to his mouth, and drank its contents down!

For an instant there was breathless silence among the British privileged guests, and then they began to whisper to one another. All that stopped, however, when Queen Victoria silently took her finger bowl in her two hands, lifted it, and drank its contents! A moment later 500 surprised British ladies and gentlemen simultaneously drank the contents of their own fingerbowls. It was the queen's uncommon courtesy guarded her guest from certain embarrassment.

"Knowledge, ability, experience are of little avail in reaching high success if courtesy be lacking," says George D. Powers. "Courtesy is the one passport that will be accepted without question in every land, in every office, in every home, in every heart in the world. For nothing commends itself so well as kindness; and courtesy is kindness." Call it what you may, courtesy is the one passport you can't be without if you intend to get where you want to go. Don't leave home without it.

Smile
What Sunshine is to Flowers

The muscles of the face are capable of over 250,000 different combinations of expressions. And one of the most useful is a smile. Fulton J. Sheen used to say, "A smile across the aisle of a bus in the morning could save a suicide later in the day." That statement is true. We all need the healing medicine "of the heart" that a smile, even from strangers, provides.

Joseph Addison put it this way: "What sunshine is to flowers, smiles are to humanity." Don't say you can't make a difference! Don't ever say you have nothing to give! Each of us can give a smile, spontaneously and sincerely. Its value may not be at once recognized, but be assured that it will be felt. A smile is a curve that can set a lot of things straight!

Smiling is infectious, you catch it like the flu,
When someone smiled at me today, I started smiling too.

I passed around the corner and someone saw my grin,
When he smiled I realized I'd passed it on to him.
I thought about that smile, then I realized its worth,
A single smile, like mine, could travel 'round the earth.
So, if you feel a smile begin, don't leave it undetected;
Let's start an epidemic quick, and get the world infected!

Job for Today and the Days to Come
Smiles are free, distribute them freely. Let the sunshine in the heart float to the face. Find occasions today, to pass along a heartfelt smile.

A Healthy Dose of Laughter, Sleep and Dreams

A merry heart doeth good like a medicine:
but a broken spirit drieth the bones.
Proverbs 17:22

A child laughs 400 times a day on the average, while an adult laughs only 15 times each day. Which is puzzling since laughter feels so good and is so good for us! You may know the benefits of laughter on the mind and spirit, but are you aware of how much a good laugh can help you physically? Norman Cousins used to say that laughter is so beneficial for your body that it is like "inner jogging."

Mayo Clinic (Mayo Clinic Health Letter, March 1993) reports that laughter aids breathing by disrupting your normal respiration pattern and increasing your breathing rate. It can even help clear mucus from your lungs. Laughter is also good for your heart. It increases circulation and improves the delivery of oxygen and nutrients to tissues throughout your body. A good laugh helps your immune system fight off colds, flu and sinus problems by increasing the concentration of immunoglobulin A in your saliva. And it may help control pain by raising the levels of certain brain chemicals (endorphins).

Furthermore, it is a natural stress reliever. Have you ever laughed so hard that you doubled over, fell off your chair or spit out your food? You cannot maintain muscle tension when you are laughing! You are allowed more than 15 laughs a day! Laughter: it's just good medicine!

Sleep

When thou liest down, thou shalt not be afraid:
yea, thou shalt lie down, and thy sleep shall be sweet.
Proverbs 3:24

Almost a third of our lifetime is spent in bed oblivious to the living world. The sleep of a labouring man is sweet. The wombed-man (woman) was created from Adam by putting him to a deep sleep. In the same way, the Bride of Christ was taken from the pierced side of Jesus that made Him taste death in His body for the sins of mankind.

Christians, as the beloved of the Lord, have the possibility of sleeping well, if we forgive everybody. For then, we can say like King David: I will both lay me down in peace and sleep; for thou Lord, only makest me to dwell in safety. When we sleep, our heart is awake, possibly also our spirit. Our reins (inner being) instruct us in the night seasons.

The lazy person desires a little more sleep and slumber, thereby inviting poverty. Joseph Cossman says that sometimes, the best bridge between despair and hope is a good night's sleep. One man rightly compares carrying care to bed as sleeping with a pack on one's back.

The Psalmist advises us to commune with our own heart upon our bed and be still before we go to sleep. Taking stock of the events of the day and the words that went forth from our mouths will enable us to obtain the censure of the Lord and receive His wisdom to be more careful with the words of our mouth in the future.

Dreams
Dreams are not all of the same kind. All have been day dreaming at some time or the other. "Pipe dreams" were the hallucinations people in certain literary circles had under the influence of opium smoked in a pipe.

"I have a dream that one day this nation will rise up and live out the true meaning of its creed: "We hold these truths to be self-evident: that all men are created equal.

I have a dream that my four children will one day live in a nation where they will not be judged by the colour of their skin but by the content of their character." These are the heroic words of Martin Luther King Jr.. His soul has entered the realm where his dream is a reality, in heaven, where inner, Christ like character is the radiance on the exterior.

The nature of dreams indicate the condition of the heart and mind, the visitation of angels, demonic powers, the symbols of prophecy, messages from the heavenly realm, the aspirations, confusions and terrors of the heart and pollutions of the flesh. Jacob, Joseph and Daniel, besides the foster parents of the child Jesus were dreamers receiving messages through angelic visitation. It is amazing that Joseph (the foster parent of Jesus) received guidance four times through dreams.

There are gateways to the soul and mind that psychology knows nothing about. Great men and ideas are driven by dreams and visions that fire the heart and mind.

Envy, Anger and Hypocrisy

Envy

A person without Christ is often full of envy, murder, debate, deceit and malignity. Wrath is cruel, anger is outrageous; but none can withstand envy. A sound heart is the life of the flesh: but envy is the rottenness of the bones. The patriarchs, moved with envy, sold Joseph into Egypt: but God was with him and the path of humiliation that they made for him was the very path of their own salvation. Pilate knew that the Jews had delivered Jesus due to envy. The priests were filled with envy when they put the apostles into the prison, when God did special miracles through Peter. The Jews were again moved by envy when they rose against Paul.

The Christian is advised by God not to let his heart envy sinners or the oppressor: not to choose any of their ways, but to be in the fear of the LORD all the day long. The best antidote for envy is to consider every person better than ourselves in some way or the other and look for that difference actively. Loving our enemy with the love of Jesus, makes it possible for us to overcome the spirit of envy.

Have you seen a man diligent in his work? He shall stand before kings; he shall not stand before mean men.
Proverbs 22:29

But we desire earnestly that each one of you show the same diligence to the full assurance of hope unto the end.
Hebrews 6:11

Anger-One Letter short of "Danger"
Anger is just one letter short of danger -- it's true in English as well as in practice. Dr. Bedford Williams at Duke University has determined that students who scored high on a "hostility test" were in far greater danger of dying young than their peers. In fact, those who were prone to anger were in greater physical danger than those who smoked, had high blood pressure or even high cholesterol.

A prayerless man is a powerless man who tends to get "worked up," "over-heated" or just plain "hopping mad." Those closest to us know it best. One little boy said, referring to his mother: "When she starts to act real weird, you have to look scared and serious. Don't giggle. When mommies are mad, they get madder when you giggle."

Staying angry is dangerous. Don't let your hostility manage you. Ambrose Bierce put it so well, "Speak when you are angry and you will make the best speech you will ever regret." Anger is the spirit of murder and the desire of satan is to lead hatred and anger to end in murder.

James Thurber advises "Let us not look back in anger, nor forward in fear, but around in awareness." The Chinese say that if you are patient in a moment of anger, you will avoid one hundred days of sorrow. E. Kenny put it even better: He who angers you, conquers you."

An angry man stirs up strife, and
a furious man abounds in transgression.
Proverbs 29:22

Hypocrisy-The Daughter of Pride

Practice What You Preach

You can know all the scriptures,
Have all the bibles you can reach,
But when push comes to shove
Do you practice what you preach?

You can yell far and wide
Proclaiming your love for Christ,
But what have you given him
When for you He gave his life?
You can lecture others
About the wrong things they do,
But before you look at others
You need to look at you.
You can memorize the bible
Know it from front to back,
But you don't use it to regulate others
Regulate how you act!
Take a good look at yourself
Not at what others do,
Because when Jesus comes to get his children ...
Will He be coming for you too?
~ Author Unknown ~

SHOW MERCY - DON'T JUDGE
Pray, don't find fault with the man that limps
Or stumbles along the road.
Unless you have worn the shoes he wears
Or struggled beneath his load.
There may be tacks in his shoes that hurt
Though hidden away from view.

Or the burden he bears, placed on your back
Might cause you to stumble too.
Don't sneer at the man who's down today
Unless you have felt the blow
That caused his fall or felt the shame
That only the fallen know.
You may be strong, but still the blows
That was his, if dealt to you
In the selfsame way, at the selfsame time
Might cause you to stagger too.
Don't be too harsh, with the man that sins
Or pelt him with word or stone
Unless you are sure - yea, doubly sure -
That you have no sins of your own.
For, If the tempter's voice should whisper as soft to you
As it did to him, when he went astray-
It might cause you to falter too.

Part Three

The Christian Life

Praying and Waiting on God

The Need for Solitude

> *And when He had sent the multitudes away,*
> *He went up on the mountain by Himself to pray.*
> *Now when evening came, He was alone there.*
> *Matthew 14:23*

One who truly loves the spouse will desire to spend much quality time with him or her. The Lord Jesus is the most approachable and available Person of Love to all who seek Him. The Lord Jesus is the Jealous God who considers it adultery if we should love the things of this world or waste our time in its trivial fancies. Modern civilization is so complex as to make the devotional life all but impossible. It wears us out by multiplying distractions and beats us down by destroying our solitude, where otherwise we might drink and renew our strength before going out to face the world again.

The thoughtful soul to solitude retires," said the poet of other and quieter times; but where is the solitude to which we can retire today? Science, which has provided men with certain material comforts, has robbed them of their souls by surrounding them with a world hostile to their existence.

"Commune with your own heart upon your bed and be still" is a wise and healing counsel, but how can it be followed in this day of the newspaper, the telephone, the radio, the television and Internet? These modern playthings, like pet tiger cubs, have grown so large and dangerous that they threaten to devour us all. What was intended to be a blessing has become a positive curse. No spot is now safe from the world's intrusion. Of God and Men, 125." If Tozer wrestled with this in his day, how much more are we bombarded today! We have all the influences of which he speaks, and much more all-pervasive, plus the internet and a host of other 'playthings' seeking to devour us. Lord, help us somehow to escape today and retire to solitude, even if only for a brief time. Amen."

Prayer-The Lifeblood of a Christian

*Every great movement of God can be
traced to a kneeling figure.*
D.L. Moody

Pray without ceasing.
II Thessalonians 5:17

God does not want, for his own sake, to be asked that His name be holy, His will good, or His rulership complete. But for our sake he wants us to pray to Him for these things, so that instead of profaning His name, resisting his will, and arrogantly asserting ourselves in rebellion against his rule, we might truly revere Him, do His will, and accept His rule. He wants us to acknowledge this. He wants us to pray, humbly admitting that our own sinfulness, stubbornness, and half-heartedness are obstacles that God has to overcome, that only He can overcome.[7]

It is only through grace that we can do the works of God. Our faith in the unmerited generosity of God fills us with love, with its insistence on action. When this happens, we come to know what an inexhaustible wealth of grace awaits all those who call on the Lord for power and new life (Ps.86:5; Rom.10:12). We know that this is a power we can never attain on our own. This drives us to pray.

Actually, God's kingdom does not depend on our praying, our preaching, or our spiritual reading. But only when he is persistently asked will he come and act, for this calling on God is the only way to express the faith that God is God and that He alone can give us what is good.

A praying Christian is the terror of Satan and well-known to God and the saints and angels in heaven. A praying Christian inhales the dew of heaven.

Travelling on My Knees

Last night I took a journey
To a land across the seas.
I didn't go by ship or plane
I travelled on my knees.
I saw so many people there
In bondage to their sin,
And Jesus told me I should go,
That there were souls to win.
But I said "Jesus, I can't go
To lands across the seas."
He answered quickly, "Yes, you can
By travelling on your knees."

He said, "You pray, I'll meet the need.
    You call, and I will hear.
    It's up to you to be concerned
    For lost souls far and near."
And so I did; knelt in prayer,
    Gave up some hours of ease,
And with the Saviour by my side,
    I travelled on my knees.
As I prayed on, I saw souls saved
    And twisted persons healed,
I saw God's workers strength renewed
    While labouring in the field.
I said, "Yes Lord, I'll take the job.
    Your heart I want to please.
I'll heed Your call and swiftly go
    By travelling on my knees."

- Author Unknown -

I exhort therefore, first of all, that
supplications, prayers, intercessions,
thanksgivings be made for all men;
    I Timothy 2:1

Waiting on God-Neither Easy nor Popular

Lead me in thy truth, and teach me: for thou art the
God of my salvation; on thee do I wait all the day.
Psalms 25:5

Rest in the LORD, and wait patiently for him:
fret not thyself because of him who prospereth in his way,
because of the man who bringeth wicked devices to pass.
Psalms 37:7

The LORD is good unto them that wait for him,
to the soul that seeketh him. It is good that a man should
both hope and quietly wait for the salvation of the LORD.
Lamentations 3:25, 26

Waiting is not something that people think about with great
sympathy. In fact, most people consider waiting a waste of
time. This is because the culture in which we live is basically
saying, "Get going! Do something! Don't just sit there and
wait!" For many, waiting is an awful desert between where
they are and where they want to go. And people do not like
such a place. They want to get out of it by doing something.
-Henri J. M. Nouwen

Waiting is difficult and unpopular because people are afraid of inner feelings, other people, the future, etc., The more afraid we are, the harder waiting becomes. People who wait have received a promise that allows them to wait. Waiting is not a movement from nothing to something, but from something to something more.

The Psalmist was weary from crying, his throat was dried up and his eyes failed in waiting for his God. Waiting is hard if we want to do the things that will make the desired events take place. Waiting becomes a radical approach to life in a world that is obsessed with controlling events. Waiting is active. A waiting person is a patient person. Waiting is open-ended. Waiting prevents us from being seduced by despair. Waiting is shaped by sensitivity to the Word. It is in constant expectancy, knowing that the Lord wants to speak to us. Marriage, friendship, community, prayer,… all have to do with waiting. The attitude of waiting helps us to live spiritually in a chaotic world.

---

7. *Eberhard Arnold, Why Pray*

True Freedom

Eberhard Arnold compares the bondage of moralism to the captive balloon that was tied to a steel cable, bound to moral law, human tenets, and iron constraint. There is no free will in it; it is legalism. He likens the gas filled balloon abandoned to wind and storm high in the atmosphere to the naïve use of the expression "free will." The crew of such a balloon are not free when their airship is carried to a desert or drowned in the sea. That so-called freedom was really dangerous instability.

Imagine a young man walking down the streets of a big city. He is surrounded by brightly lit advertising. Movie theatres, music halls, cabarets, and taverns lure him. Women accost him. An excited political mob tries to incite him to murder. Impurity and bloodshed, lying and deceit surround him like winds blowing from all sides. Darkness settles over his heart. The true face of things is veiled. He succumbs to the great delusion of corrupt and uncontrolled life.

If this young man suddenly decides to obey one of these winds, does that make him free? Was it his free will acting? He may say yes, and even if he regrets it later, he may still think that he did what he wanted to do. Possibly. No doubt he was free to do evil. But he was not free to do good when he did things that later caused him remorse. It certainly was will, but it was not free will. His will was just as badly enslaved and subjugated as the free balloon drifting out over sea or desert. The modern airplane can illustrate for us what true freedom guided by the Holy Spirit is.

Marriage and Family

The family that prays together, stays together.
Anon

Marriage for a Christian couple must have the approval and blessing of the parents (if they are Christian) as well as the local church. Dating, pre-, and extra-marital sex are not permitted by the Word of God.

The perfect plan of God is for one man to have one wife, to become one flesh, through a whole lifetime in fellowship with God, conjugality and mutual care and honour. The family is to serve the church and the world. The God of Holiness hates homosexuality, polygamy, and promiscuity. Jesus condemned adultery even in a lustful look and the evil desire of the heart.

Divorce is permitted only in the case of adultery. Remarriage in such a case, though common today, was not permitted by most of the church fathers (leaders upto

5th cent.). Cohabitation and lack of marital obligation are causing whole generations to suffer loneliness, disorientation and lack of spiritual content in life. Women rebel against the inconvenience of pregnancy and the pain of birth, and men rebel against the burden of commitment to the children they father and to the woman who bears them. The media and liberal education are lowering the threshold of age and impulse for sexual activity.

Although headship is vested in the man, obedience and submission are first required in both husband and wife towards God and then to each other in the truth. Love and humility will rule in the house of prayer and the family unit is truly blessed in the greater unity of the church. A marriage needs a whole lifetime to grow and mature. Satan hates this divine institution and desires to split the family and the church, as much as God wants to bless and prosper them. Marriage and the family are institutions that are threatened as never before. A record number of children worldwide are being born out of wedlock. In the U.S., nearly 40 percent of births were to unmarried women in 2007, compared with about 34 percent in 2002.

In the U.K., single women and lesbian couples won parental rights in 2008, removing the requirement that fertility clinics consider a child's need for a father. Marriage rates in England and Wales have fallen to the lowest level since records began in 1862. Love and faithfulness are truths that are immortal and eternal. God's laws for marriage and family are made to reflect these truths. Even people caught up in lustful relationships, gay, lesbian or heterosexual find a craving for faithfulness from their partner.

The Bible does not mince words in declaring the truths for all time, every society and civilization. We are living in a world today that is turning upside down in a satanic bid to rebel against God and His laws. Satan and his demons have filled the world with lies, manipulating men, women and children to such an extent that truth seems to be a lie and lie seems to be truth.

The Church

*"Upon This Rock will I build my church and
the gates of hell shall not prevail against it."
-Jesus Christ*

The building, the denomination, the congregation, the believer, the body of Christ, the numerous fallen churches with fallen doctrines, and the cults are all called churches. But there is only One mystical, universal body of Christ made up of spirit-baptised individual believers that can be called as church. The historical 'religion' has however perverted the understanding to refer to buildings and denominations.

The Early Christians had a communal way of life and shared their wealth and resources in such a manner that they turned the world upside down and the people of the world said: See how they love each other! The Catholic Church tries to claim direct descent from these Christians, but a religion where there are 100 bodyguards for the Pope is a mockery of the Man of Galilee and the Son of God who healed his enemies. The Bible is the Word of God and basis of faith for the Church. The keys of the kingdom of heaven are given to every believer and the gates of hell cannot prevail against the Church of Jesus Christ. The fountain of water and blood that flowed from the pierced side of Jesus will wash and present the Church blameless and holy before the Throne of God. The Church of Christ is another name for the heavenly city- New Jerusalem and Zion, the Bride of Christ will display the glorious wisdom and mercy of God through all ages.

True Worship

Man was made to worship God. Everything else will only frustrate the purpose and satisfaction of man. Every man worships something or the other. The Lord Jesus predicted the spreading of true worship of the Father in spirit and truth beyond the confines of space, time and Jewry to all nations.

God is Good and transforms all who worship Him, like Himself. Satan is Evil and makes all that worship him directly or indirectly, evil as himself. The eternity of the redeemed Christian will be spent in the most satisfying activity namely, worshipping God. The desire for knowing God and worshipping Him is latent in the spirit of man and released by the Holy Spirit. Fallen flesh and the unsanctified heart war against this desire of the spirit. Those who worship God acknowledge Truth in all its beauty. The worship of the Living God is to be done in the beauty of holiness, decently and in order, not with showmanship or glorifying musical or vocal skills of man.

Meditation: Let us consider our daily habits. What do we occupy most of our time with? That will determine the colour of our character. We become transformed into the very character of what we worship.

> *Give unto the LORD the glory due unto his name:*
> *bring an offering, and come before him:*
> *worship the LORD in the beauty of holiness.*
> *1 Chronicles 16:29*

Jesus was not a long haired Nazarite.
He was a Nazarene.

Jesus is often portrayed in pictures as a blonde hippie with blue eyes. This is the lie of the western religion. Jesus does not want us to make or worship any pictures of Him. He is able to change His appearance. The Beauty of Jesus is the Beauty of His Character. His Name is His Character and Authority. It grieves God when humans cannot accept the form of their own face, skin, hair or eye colour. Jesus loves the people of all religions, ethnic groups, cultures and languages-not only Christians. The Gospel of Christ is timeless.

Modesty in Dress is required of all God's Children

> *The woman shall not wear that which pertaineth*
> *unto a man, neither shall a man put on a woman's*
> *garment; for all that do so are abomination unto the*
> *Lord, thy God.*
> *Deuteronomy 22:5*

Christian men and women know that God looks at the heart and hence seek to decorate their inner being with good works and a meek and quiet spirit. A fair woman without discretion is compared to a jewel on the snout of a pig. Jewellery and expensive garments are not for the God-fearing woman. The world and its fashions, lusts and pleasures pass away. The Word and they that do the Will of God abide forever.

Hair and Head Coverings

On an average, we grow 40-80 metres of hair daily, because the 100-200,000 hairs on our head add 0.4 mm to each hair. Men are to maintain their hair short, as even nature teaches that it is shame for a man to have long hair. Men are not to tonsure their heads or, colour or decorate their hair any way. Except for bald headed men, men are not to cover their head in public worship, unlike the Jewish tradition. Though it is possible that Jesus and Paul followed the Jewish tradition in the temple, Paul brings in a new ordinance to the Christian assembly by revelation from God.

Women are not to crop their hair, nor braid (make plaits), decorate or colour it. Their hair is given them for a covering. Women are required to cover their head as a sign of submission to their head-their husbands, in prayer, prophecy and worship, because of the angels. If they do not do so, they appear shamefully tonsured (hairless) before God (in worship).

Paul's commands to the Church are valid from his days until the Rapture in all the churches of God that worship the Father in spirit and truth. The equivalence made by Paul is the comparison of God being the head of Christ. It is a sign required by the angels, because God is holy. It is no Corinthian cultural relic, as western churches have conveniently interpreted it to be, due to their submission to, and integration of, devilish ideas of women´s liberation and modern worldly fashions and trends.

Diligence Vs. Negligence

Negligence is the rust of the soul,
that corrodes through all her best resolves
-Owen Feltham

How shall we escape if we neglect so great a salvation
which at the first began to be spoken by the Lord and was
confirmed unto us by them that heard him.
Hebrews 2:3

The secret of success is constancy of purpose.
-Benjamin Disraeli

The ancient Egyptians in mummifying a corpse discarded the brain but retained and highly regarded the heart. Though a dead heart is of no value, it is no wonder, as the Lord commands us to keep our heart with all diligence as it is the fountain of life.

The throne of the heart with the Spirit of Jesus ruling from it is to be carefully and diligently kept from being toppled by the flesh, Satan and the world. Strange desires, apparently harmless distractions and idle talk will prevent the constant perception of the presence of Jesus in the heart, leading us astray as circumstances are engineered by Satan. Salvation in the heart and the fear of the Lord in the mind are to be diligently maintained and guarded. We are warned to be diligent in forgiving others to be delivered from Satan. If we diligently make sure of our calling and election, we will never fall.

Fasting
True Christian Discipline

When you fast, anoint your head and wash your face so that you do not appear to others to be fasting, but to your Father, who is in the secret place; and your Father, who sees in secret, will reward you openly.
Jesus Christ, The Son of God

The Christ of God started His ministry hungering and ended it thirsting.
Maafa Dalit

More than 61% of U.S. adults and 13% of adolescents currently meet the scientific definition of obesity, with some 300,000 Americans dying each year from health problems directly related to obesity. This is probably the most sedentary generation of people in the history of the world!

Fasting is also a form of solidarity with the starving.

In the western world, filled with gluttony and unhealthy eating habits, this discipline is badly neglected among many Christians. The rich man in the narration of Jesus of a true story, was having sumptuous food everyday while his fellow human, the beggar at his gate was starving to death. The judgement is terrible, eternal flames and torment.

Jesus said that when He would leave the midst of His disciples that the children of the bride chamber will fast. Paul spoke of being often in fastings. Fasting brings the craving of the taste and the whining of the stomach under control. The time set apart in scripture meditation and prayer will be greatly blessed if we come to the Lord with an empty stomach. Fasting puts the regular punctuation to the secular life of a Christian that is needed to give God, His Word and prayer, the place they deserve. Clearly, the pleasures of eating are fleeting, whereas the pleasures of fasting are lasting.

Dieting and Fasting

While visiting a family, a pastor was describing the benefits of fasting. I'm on a diet," butts in the daughter of the family. "I, too, eat only once a day. What's the big deal?" "My child, you diet to make your body pleasing to yourself and to others," responded the pastor quietly. "The Christian fasts to make the soul pleasing to God."

*Discipleship is more than getting to know what the
Teacher knows, it is getting to be what He is.*
Juan Carlos Ortiz

Fasting and Prayer will terrorise the devil.
Maafa Dalit

*Christ did no sin, knew no sin, in Him was no sin,
Yet he fasted.
How much more do I need to fast!
Maafa Dalit*

The Furnace of Suffering

For this is thankworthy, if a man for conscience toward God endure grief, suffering wrongfully.
1 Peter 2:19

...when he has tried me, I shall come forth as gold.
Job 23:10

That the trial of your faith, being much more precious than of gold that perishes, though it be tried with fire, might be found unto praise and honour and glory at the appearing of Jesus Christ.
1 Peter 1:7

Those who have seen paddy transplantation, will know that the seedling is uprooted, taken off the water bed, and left on dry soil for two or three days. If the plant has any sensitivity, and it has, it will feel a sense of threat to life when the roots start to dry. When it is replanted into the soil, it sends roots deep down into the soil with double vigour. The plant grows and yields sometimes eight to ten times as much rice as a plant that was not transplanted.

Philip Berrigan in The Way of the Cross says: Discipleship is the way of the cross. And the cross has a distinct meaning for us. It means punishment by the State for dissent, especially civil resistance, wherein man's unjust law is broken to keep God's law. It meant execution for Jesus, as it often does in the poor World. It often means torture and punishment. That is what modern Christians fear –the cross. The disciples feared what the Romans did to zealots and troublemakers-their crosses dotted the landscape.

Few have suffered as righteous Job who, after the loss of children, property and health, gave the true representation of God to his friends and found his suffering healed and state restored to greater blessing when he interceded for his friends. Sickness, poverty, death of loved ones, sudden calamity and evil strike in the most perplexing way and raise heart rending and questioning cries. The answer eluded Job until he was vindicated. God found his servant worthy of His Name through all the trials that Satan was permitted to bring. God loves you and will answer your questions completely and finally, if you trust in Jesus.

Calvary is God's great proof
that suffering in the will of God
always leads to glory.
Warren Wiersbe

Pain and suffering are not necessarily the sign of God's
anger; they may be exactly the opposite.
Anon

TV and Internet
The Satanic Hypnosis

But thou, O man of God, flee these things; and follow after righteousness, godliness, faith, love, patience, meekness.
1 Timothy 6:11

Redeeming the time, because the days are evil.
Ephesians 5:16

Wherefore, my dearly beloved, flee from idolatry.
1Corinthians 10:14

Hell and destruction have opened their mouth wide and people instead of running in the opposite direction, are heading straight into it. Two of the most powerful tools that Satan is using to increase the citizenry in hell are Television and Internet.

Billions sit glued to their stupid TV sets every day, while Internet, though providing useful and rapid international communication, is blinding 100s of millions of people to the eternal purpose of their existence. Many Christian families have the TV icon as the centre of orbit of their family life and not prayer, worship and bible reading. For many people unwinding from the pressure of modern living means killing time at the magic box.

The violent, empty and filthy images and words of ungodly people pours into the brains and minds of people who ensure church attendance Sunday after Sunday. To make matters worse, so called ministers of Christ also have the TV monster in their homes.

Let Jesus from My Heart
Bless the world through my Speech, Works and Ways

I beseech you therefore, brethren, by the mercies of God, that you present your bodies a living sacrifice, holy, acceptable unto God, which is your reasonable service.
Romans 12:1

Eyes of the Lord, Eye of Man and The Evil Eye
The eyes of the Lord are in every place beholding the good and the evil. The Lord guides and directs His children with His Eye. The eye of man is the lamp of his body. If his eye is single, his whole body shall be full of light. If the light (knowledge) in a man be darkness, how great is that darkness. Hordes of evil demons, messengers of Satan seek out every soul on earth, with their evil eyes, to steal, kill, and pollute. Their strategies and schemes are daily aimed to separate Christians from fellowship with the light of God and His living Word.

Speech-Taming The Tongue

> *And the tongue is a fire, a world of iniquity:*
> *so is the tongue among our members, that it defiles*
> *the whole body, and sets on fire the course of nature;*
> *and it is set on fire of hell.*
> *For every kind of beasts, ...and of birds, and of serpents, ...*
> *.. is tamed, and have been tamed of mankind: But the*
> *tongue can no man tame; it is an unruly evil,*
> *full of deadly poison.*
> *James 3:6-8*

Our words will justify us or condemn us. Jesus also said that we will have to give account of even our idle words. He knew what He was talking about, being the very Word of God. In a multitude of words there lacks no evil. A fool is full of words. There is more hope for a fool than for one who answers a matter before he hears it. James follows up to call the tongue an unruly evil! Modern neurology reveals that the speech centre of the brain has an overarching influence on all other centres.

An ill tongue to an angry heart is what fuel is to fire. But the tongue of the Christian, according to the Bible, ministers grace to the hearers, speaks wholesome words, is a ready writer, has no deceit and is like choice silver or a tree of life. Life and death are in the power of the tongue. The tongue is connected to the heart, and what the heart overflows with, finds expression in speech. What comes out of the mouth are what are truly defiling and reveals the heart of the speaker. The pharisaic modern world is very occupied with cleanness and hygiene, but condones swearing, evil speaking and gossiping. A child of God is slow to anger, slow to speak, but quick to listen.

The spirit-filled Christian is recognised by his gentleness, quietness and the grace of speech, all brought about by the Holy Spirit who through glossolalia (unknown tongues) tames the tongue and makes it praise its Creator.

Ears that Hear the Word

The circumcision of the New Testament Israelite is not in the flesh, but in the heart and ears of the inward being so that the Christian walks by faith by listening to the voice of God that tells the way on every side. The ear that hears reproof abides among the wise. The young man must beware of the words of the strange woman though they drop honey, and sound smoother than oil.

The ears must be open to the cry of the poor and oppressed and to the reading and hearing of the law, otherwise God will turn a deaf ear to our prayer. The ear of the sinful man is not satisfied with hearing, nor the eye with seeing and the soul of man cannot be satisfied even it gets the whole universe. Satisfaction is in knowing God. God who planted the eyes and ears has infinite understanding. The wise man inclines his ear and seeks knowledge.

Hands to Bless

Hands speak of works. When Jesus took the nails through His wrists the handwriting of the law condemning men was taken out of the way and nailed to the Cross of Christ. Hence, no amount of religious works will save the soul of man. Only one who has a pure heart and clean hands can ascend to the hill of Mount Zion in heaven. By the works of the law shall no man be justified. The Christian is called to abide in the death of Christ so that the life-giving grace of Christ may also manifest itself. The right hand of the sinner is one of falsehood, with mischief and bribes.

Considering the biological fact that there are 72 feet of nerve fibre on each square inch of our hands, it is not surprising that blessing is communicated through laying on of hands. Jesus is the Right Hand of God- the Power and Majesty of God. Shaking hands in western tradition was used to confirm a deal, but also originally meant to show that you have no weapon in that hand. The evil eye is also believed to be communicated through handshakes.

Hand fasting or tying the right hands together at the wrists was once used to confirm a wedding covenant.

Feet that Walk in His Ways

God wants us to ponder the path of our feet because He sees all our ways and numbers all our steps. A sinner's feet are always hasty. The God-fearing man is urged to turn not to the right hand or left, but to remove the foot from evil.

The feet of them that bring the gospel are beautiful in the eyes of God. One who flatters his neighbour spreads a net for his feet. It is better, as with the hands, to mortify and make the feet lifeless to sin, than enter hellfire with both feet. The Lord will order the steps of the righteous. The gospel of God is so serious that the dust shaken off from the feet of them who proclaim it, can testify against those who reject the gospel. The righteous man must beware of the strange woman whose feet go down to death and her steps take hold of hell.

The nail went through the feet of Jesus as the penalty for the sins of our evil ways. Now the feet of Jesus burns brightly like brass in judgement against those who reject Him and do not turn from their sins. Jesus washed the feet of His disciples to show the extent to which humility is required from us not to look down on anybody, but always be prepared to intercede for the forgiveness of the transgressions of our brothers and sisters.

How to become a beautiful Christian

*For **Attractive Lips** Speak words of kindness*
*For **Beautiful Eyes** Look for good in others*
*To lose **Weight**, Let go of stress, hatred, discontentment*
and the need to control others
*To improve your **Ears***
Listen to the Word of God
*For **Poise** walk with knowledge and self-esteem*
*To strengthen your **Arms***
Hug at least 3 people each day
Touch someone with your love
*To strengthen your **Heart***
Forgive yourself and others
*For the ultimate in **business, casual or evening attire***
Put on the robe of Christ.
It fits like a glove, but allows room for growth.
Doing these things on a daily basis,
will make me an even more beautiful person.

I am a beautiful gift from heaven.

Learn from yesterday,
live for TODAY,
hope for tomorrow

Today I will delete from my Diary two days:
yesterday and tomorrow.
Yesterday was to learn and tomorrow will be the consequence
of what I did and left undone today.
Today I will face life with the conviction that
this day will not ever return.
Today is the last opportunity I have to live intensely,
as no one can assure me that I will see tomorrow's sunrise.
Today I will be brave enough not to let
any opportunity pass me by.
Today I will invest my most valuable resource:
my time, in the most transcendental work: my life;
I will spend each minute passionately to make
of today a different and unique day.

Christian Courage

But you shall receive power, after that the Holy Ghost is
come upon you: and ye shall be (martyrs) witnesses unto me
both in Jerusalem, and in all Judea, and in Samaria, and
unto the uttermost part of the earth.
Acts of the Apostles 1:8

The communist Party boss promised the post world
war II clergy that the government would pay them
from tax revenues, if communism and Christianity
worked together. Most of the audience cheered and one
church leader promised that the clergy would cooperate.
Richard Wurmbrand did not cheer. He had already been
imprisoned and beaten several times for his faith. He knew
that speaking out again could cost him his freedom. His
wife, Sabrina, sitting beside him, said: "Go and wash this
shame from the face of Christ" she demanded.

Gathering courage, Richard asked permission to speak

and was welcomed forward by the organisers who expected a unity speech. Instead, Richard began by saying it was the duty of ministers to glorify God, not earthly powers. He encouraged the clergy to support the eternal kingdom of God, not the powers of Romania. As he continued, someone began to clap, and then another, and soon there erupted waves of applause. Stop! Your right to speak has been withdrawn. "My right to speak comes from God," declared Richard. He kept speaking until his microphone was disconnected. The courage of the Christian is tested in his boldness to confess Christ to the ungodly and the worldly wise.

Covetousness and Contentment

Love not the world, neither the things that are in the world. If any man love the world, the love of the Father is not in him -John The Apostle

And when the woman saw that the tree was good for food, that it was pleasant to the eyes,... she took of the fruit...did eat, and gave also unto her husband with her. ; and he did eat. And the eyes of them both were opened.   Genesis 3:6,7

More than a 1000 billion dollars (one trillion) are spent every year in the mammoth, global, advertisement business. Experimental results confirm the fact that advertisements featuring attractive women seduce men into parting with their money. The marketing people are fully aware of that. Says Brennan Manning: "The spirituality of Bethlehem is simply incomprehensible to the advertising industry. The opening notes of Beethoven's Fifth Symphony are being used to sell us pain reliever, and the prayer of St. Francis is being used to sell us hair conditioner."

Men, women and children are deceived into buying up unwanted gadgets, toys and vanities by the glamour of the ad industry. Pornography is reaching catastrophic dimensions destroying marriages and families in a rapidly modernizing world enslaving men through their eyes. Women like to do window shopping of all the glories of the world that their money cannot buy. The constant bombarding of the advertisement industry makes the woman feel thoroughly inadequate before the mirror and her peers. No amount of the endless miles of dresses, facials and handbags will clear the emotional deficit. Contentment comes from knowing that my soul is deeply loved and cherished by my Lord and Saviour. The ornaments of holy women in the New Testament belong to the inner being: good works, sobriety and a quiet spirit. The Christians are a peculiar people zealous of good works showing the light of the Father.

The Attitude of Gratitude

> *When you arise in the morning, give thanks for the morning light. Give thanks for your life and strength. Give thanks for your food and for the joy of living.*

And if perchance you see no reason for giving thanks,
rest assured the fault is in yourself."
-Ascribed to Chief Tecumseh

Gratitude is cultivated in hearts that take time to
count up past mercies.
Charles E. Jefferson

The late Dr. Fulton Oursler used to tell of an old woman who took care of him when he was a child. Anna was a former slave who, after emancipa-tion, was hired by the family for many years. He remembered her sitting at the kitchen table, her hands folded and her eyes gazing upward as she prayed, "Much obliged, Lord, for my vittles." He asked her what vittles were and she replied that they were food and drink. He told her that she would get food and drink whether or not she gave thanks, and Anna said, "Yes, we'll get our vittles, but it makes 'em taste better when we're thankful." She told him that an old preacher taught her, as a little girl, to always look for things to be grateful for. So, as soon as she awoke each morning, she asked herself, "What is the first thing I can be grateful for today?" Sometimes the smell of early-morning coffee prompted her to say, "Much obliged, Lord, for the coffee. And much obliged, too, for the smell of it!"

Young Fulton grew up and left home. One day he returned home following a message that Anna was dying. He found her in bed with her hands folded over her white sheets, just as he had seen them folded in prayer over her white apron at the kitchen table so many times before. He wondered what she could give thanks for at a time like this. As if reading his mind, she opened her eyes and gazed at the loving faces around her bed, she said quietly, "Much obliged, Lord, for such fine friends" and closing her eyes, slipped away to be with the Lord.

Contentment makes poor men rich,
Discontentment makes rich men poor
Benjamin Franklin

The holy person is the only contented person in the world.
William Gurnall

The world provides enough for every man's need,
but not enough for one man's greed.
Mahatma Gandhi

Godliness + Contentment = Great Gain

For we have brought nothing into the world: it is manifest

that neither can we carry anything out. But having
sustenance and covering, we will be content with these.
I Timothy 6:6-8

Complaints drive away Contentment

Two survivors of shipwreck managed to swim to a small island on which nothing but a huge tree grew. Standing in the middle of the island, the beautiful tree gave them food and sheltered them from the sun and rain. At night they lay on leaves that cushioned their backs from the cold earth. When their clothes wore out, they fashioned some simple covering from barks and leaves.

However, as the days passed, they got used to the tree that they started finding fault with it. "All we have is this stupid tree!" they grumbled. Or one of them would murmur, "I wish we had something better!" Unknown to them, every complaint they uttered caused the tree to wither a little. After a few months, the tree died, leaving the two with neither food nor shade.

Contentment makes poor men rich and discontentment makes rich men poor. The wealthiest man is he who is contented with least. The Christian is called upon to make his material possessions immaterial. Let your riches consist not in the largeness of your possessions but in the fewness of wants. The Bible teaches us to be content with what we have, not with what we are. Charity gives itself rich. Covetousness or dry drunkenness, hoards itself poor. The soul of man is infinite in what it covets. Francis Xavier said that he heard many confessions, but never one of covetousness!

Mammon-The God of this World

But those who desire to be rich fall into temptation and a snare, and many unwise and hurtful lusts, which plunge men into destruction and ruin. For the love of money is the root of every evil; which some having aspired after, have wandered from the faith, and pierced themselves with many sorrows. I Timothy 6:9,10

From cowries to gold and silver coins, to paper money, cheques, plastic cards and the blip on a computer screen, money is the elusive commodity for which sweat and labour are paid. The rule of this world is: "He who makes the gold, makes the rules." The Bible call money as the god of this world and the love for money as the root of all evil". Money is the (unfair) exchange of the combined elements of production--land, capital, and labour. Hence, Jesus called it unrighteous mammon.

Tom Potts, a Quaker wrote: "America has been taken

over by the military. They get over 60% of an overwhelming budget." Switzerland with less than 0.03 per cent of the world's population, the world's third largest financial power, houses a third of the world's private fortune, an estimated USD 2,500 billion. And then a whole science of development aid is built up to prop up the myth that the wealthy are generous. A person living in the cash economy of this world is either a worshipper of the One True Living God, the Father of Our Lord Jesus Christ or of the Golden Image of Mammon. The pure gold like glass will be under our feet in heaven which should mean that God will bring all our material desires under our feet in this life and grant us heavenly affections in preparation for the life to come. Money may be needed also by Christians to bless many, but it is a source of much sorrow and suffering in this world of wicked men.

Consumed by Materialism

When they were filled, he said unto his disciples,
Gather up the fragments that remain, that nothing be lost.
John 6:12

Kitchen gadgets, computers, audio, video and fitness equipment, besides flashy cars and a million other useless things clutter up the life of people who live like so many fools, without time for God, our fellow men, parents, neighbours. What does a person need–really need? A few pounds of food each day, heat and shelter, six feet to lie down in–and some form of working activity that will yield a sense of accomplishment. That's all–in the material sense. We are brainwashed by our economic system and buried beneath a pyramid of time payments, mortgages, preposterous gadgetry, playthings that divert our attention from the sheer idiocy of the charade. Which shall it be: bankruptcy of purse or bankruptcy of life?[8]

---

8. *Sterling Hayden, Material Needs: The Bruderhof*

Pagan Customs in Christianity

Lent, the 40 day fast preceding Easter was introduced into Christianity by the Roman Catholic Church about the year 525 A.D. This custom of abstinence and fast existed in pagan religions like the Yezidis of Kurdistan, pagan Mexicans, Egyptian Lent in honour of Adonis or Osiris. In Babylon, the fast commemorated the death and resurrection of Tammuz. Lent was observed in Assyria and Palestine in June.

Good Friday is an invention to profit the fleshly and emotional needs of the Pope of Rome. Jesus was crucified on a Wednesday and He rose from the dead soon after sunset on Saturday. The body of Christ lay in the grave for 72 hours or 3 whole days and 3 whole nights, as Jonah was in the belly of the fish for 3 days and 3 nights. (Matt.12:40; Mark 8:31; Matt.27:63; I Cor.15:4).

Easter is derived by the Roman church from the Babylonian goddess Astarte ca. 450 A.D. The Christians observed a quiet Pasch or Passover. There was no annual observance of the resurrection of Christ. The death of Christ was remembered at the Lord's table on the first day of every week (Acts 20:7). The Risen Christ is in the midst of His children every day.

Christmas is a mixture of Jo Saturnalia, a Roman festival and December 25th was sacred for the religion called Mithraism. The tree, the gifts, the lights, the dance around the tree, Santa Claus etc., are inventions of the western world that are marked by drunkenness and commercialism.

He is Risen!

The path of the just is as a shining light
That shines brighter and brighter unto the perfect day.
Proverbs 4:18

And as they walked together communing
among themselves, Jesus joined them in the Way.

Surely, O my soul, He joins thee
as you commune with yourself,
as you believe, as you read His Word,
The Blessed Report-
He is Risen !

- Maafa Dalit -

Some of the Things Jesus Created

Everything Good out of Nothing

The universe billions of light years across
The confines of which are not discovered yet!

As Jesus of Nazareth,
in the days of His flesh

He created
Tons of food for hungry people
Brand new limbs, eyes, minds and hearts,
Life and flesh to decayed corpses, leprous bodies,
Peace on stormy waters and troubled lives.
Jealousy and spite in hypocrites,
and the rulers of this age.

But above all-
He is creating…
a whole new people,
a city with foundations
for the coming eternity-
Truly free and Truly fair.

Maafa: KiSwahili for Horror or Holocaust. Europe is yet to compensate and reconcile with Africa for the 24-30 million slaves that were plundered in the depopulation of Africa in the Transatlantic Slave Trade during the so-called period of Enlightenment in Europe! Denmark accounted for 200,000 African souls in this horrendous trade.

The children of slaves and their produce are now being kept out of Europe and North America, while the cotton, cane sugar, coffee, cocoa, bananas etc., are imported at grossly unfair prices, besides the evil subsidies given by the OECD to cotton, sugar, rice, etc., The fence around the European Union is so effective that people are falling from airplanes, getting choked in trucks and crossing the Sahara in vain.

Dalit: The oppression of the ex-untouchables, over 250 million dalits, besides the over 70 million adivasis (first dwellers) in South Asia, calls for another liberation. The caste system consists of the brahmin priests, rulers, merchants and workers. The oppression of the untouchables outside the caste spectrum is based on an upward scale of awe and downward scale of contempt.

May Europe be reconciled with Africa.
May the Dalits of South Asia find true freedom.
May all men be free in knowing Truth that God is Love.

Pilgrim Ministry
www.freewebs.com/maafadalit